# Praise for *Ma*

*Point yourself to happiness.*™

# MANIFESTING
## 1·2·3

### and you don't need #3

## KEN ELLIOTT

How thought works and
the simple tools to create the
desires of your lifetime

Solace Press
Castle Rock, Colorado

Solace Press
5282 Red Pass Way
Castle Rock, CO 80108

Developmental Editor: Janice Brewster, www.creativegirlfriendspress.com
Book Designer: Karen Sulmonetti, www.sulmonettidesign.com

# Dedication

I am the result of countless kindnesses and hurts. I have been influenced by many close to me and strangers at great distances. We float in a sea of influences and I am thankful for everyone and everything that has brought me to this page at this moment. I cherish you all.

I mention just two of my many teachers here. They were instrumental in sharing their experiences and teaching me to fly on my own. They are both great teachers, pioneers and individuals with great abilities. To Judy Goodman and William Buhlman, I am honored to follow in your footsteps and this book is dedicated to you both.

# Table of Contents

Introduction: It's in Your Hands. . . . . . . . . . . . . . . . . . . . . . . . . . . 9

Chapter 1. Gratefulness as Power: Thought as a Force . . . . . . . . 14

Chapter 2. First Adventures: The Rose and a Duck . . . . . . . . . . . 21

Chapter 3. Manifesting in Real Time: Thoughts and Lists . . . . . . . 31

Chapter 4. Manifesting #1: A Key to the Kingdom . . . . . . . . . . . 40

Chapter 5. In Your Movie: Your Future Scripted and Directed by You . . 49

Chapter 6. Manifesting #2: Worry and Your Words . . . . . . . . . . . 79

Chapter 7. And You Don't Need #3: Who You Really Are . . . . . . . . 87

Chapter 8. Get Ready: It Is Already Happening . . . . . . . . . . . . . . 92

Chapter 9. The Bonus: Grateful Things . . . . . . . . . . . . . . . . . . . 101

Chapter 10. Before You Take Off: Useful Bits . . . . . . . . . . . . . . . 107

Notes and resources. . . . . . . . . . . . . . . . . . . . . . . . . . . . . . . . 144

Acknowledgements . . . . . . . . . . . . . . . . . . . . . . . . . . . . . . . . 154

About the Author . . . . . . . . . . . . . . . . . . . . . . . . . . . . . . . . . . 155

# INTRODUCTION

## It's In Your Hands

Consider what your life would be if everything you thought, imagined or hoped for simply began to materialize right in front of you. You would be the Genie, capable of anything on demand. You would have limitless opportunities and you would use your gift to fashion a fulfilling and comfortable life for yourself. Just by thinking, you would make it so.

But this is what you are already doing. Your thoughts are molding things and concepts around you constantly. You are that amazing and powerful person and everyone was born that way. This is the truth at the core of this book. Your thoughts are creating things and concepts around you constantly.

This changes everything.

**What would you like to have in your life?**
**How would you script your life if you had the chance?**
**What are your wishes?**
**Do you long for better?**

In a very short time, you will have the basic tools to answer these questions and create the dreams you seek.

This is not a long-winded book written as high literature. It is a simple guide in plain language that will quickly empower you to make marvelous changes in your life. It is my intention that these basic suggestions become your go-to manual, the simplest way to be where you wish to be.

I am very fortunate; I learned how to create changes in my life with a considerable amount of hands-on experience and from two very close friends who shared their directly observed experiences with me over many years.

The information I gleaned from these teachers is so simple it is laughable. It can seem unbelievable that something so basic and clear would produce such extraordinary results. A number of true stories are included here to clarify concepts and for your encouragement.

This is a results-oriented book, so I'm not going to get into the speculative and theoretical physics that explain the possible mechanisms at work here. Let's not discuss how the television works. Just turn it on!

Over and over, people tell me about their successes with manifesting. They say, "It just works!"

Before we begin, let's imagine a world where some of the laws of nature operate randomly or in an undependable way. In this world, you use something like a seatbelt to secure yourself into your bed. Why? Because between sundown and sunup, gravity sometimes weakens, allowing people and things to start floating around. Your life is full of gadgets to secure everything around you in the event of these gravity fluctuations.

In this unpredictable world, light switches are very problematic as well. You just never know if they're going to work correctly or not. The lights don't turn on every time you flick the switch. The brightest engineers have no control over this electrical irregularity, so you keep a lot of very big battery packs around. People pray and create all manner of ceremonies in the hope that electricity will flow to their homes properly.

Fortunately, this is not our world: We have fundamental laws of nature that constantly work. We can rely on these laws and since we understand them to a reasonable degree, we can use them to our benefit.

The discovery of a natural law or something fundamentally new is a rare occurrence. What is being offered in this book is one of those singular and important pieces of information. You will learn how thought works and you will be shown how it forms and the way it builds.

All thoughts. Your thoughts.

Your thoughts create virtually every object and concept around you. This is incredibly important to know because what you are thinking directs the path of your life.

This book is the basic instruction manual explaining for the first time how your thoughts actually take form and how to best use this remarkable tool. It is your birthright and your great gift. This information is central to your life, tremendously important and exquisitely simple. Everything in the room around you was first a thought before it came into physical form. Thoughts are what happen first, they are the primary tools that make the objects and concepts in our physical world.

Once again, gravity is a natural law and it simply pulls things to the ground. Always.

Thought is a natural law as well, building objects or concepts as you imagine them. This will be clearly demonstrated to you later in the book.

You will like this: It doesn't matter if you believe this concept or not. Your thoughts will continue to create anyway.

Pick up a coffee cup or this book. Hold it out to your side and let it go. It will go to the ground every time. Did you ever consider how thoroughly you understand gravity? Have you been amazing your friends with your mastery of gravity, grabbing their things and crashing them to the floor?

Of course not. You never heard anybody say, "Watch this! I'm really good at gravity." You understand gravity as a law and take it for granted. You and the strongest person on the planet are equals at harnessing gravity. It doesn't matter if you believe in gravity or not. Water running downhill is not dependent upon your understanding of gravity, religion or belief system.

People have been writing about the power of thought for a very long time. It is at the core of all manner of manifesting, laws of attraction, mind-power and self-help books. The premise is that your thoughts build your reality. Virtually everyone has experienced thinking of something or someone and shockingly, that person or thing appears.

Coincidences abound; it's simple probability, but sometimes what appears is beyond the odds and common sense.

We don't know how these remarkable events occur, so theories are proposed. For years, people have discussed and collected thousands of stories speculating on the cause and effect of our thoughts. There have been uncountable conversations, books and lectures on the topic.

Most of the consensus thinking that emerges is valuable and good advice. Think and speak positively. Imagine what you desire consistently and somehow stop or diminish the fear in your life. The premise is to set positive goals in your mind and follow that good advice every day for the best results. Then we hope and pray.... and wait.

No longer.

Back to the light switch. Before flipping the switch, you don't petition and hope for the lights to work. You understand that the switch is wired into the power plant and it keeps you in a constant supply of electricity.

Further, did you wake in the morning and ask permission to breathe? Did you have to study and learn where to find the best air in order to survive? No. You were born breathing and the air you require is in abundance around us all.

So as you go forward here, keep this in mind. You have been creating things with your thoughts all your life. Your thoughts create just as perfectly and powerfully as the next person's. You don't have to be expert, gifted or a believer to be a success at manifesting. Since it is your birthright, you were born breathing and manifesting like an expert.

If that is true, what would you really like to create next in your life? Let's find out.

# ONE

## Gratefulness as Power: Thought as a Force

**This is a book about asking and manifesting. But more importantly it's a book about the power of being grateful.**

I am underscoring the importance of gratefulness and love right here at the beginning. We can manifest anything with our thoughts in a positive way or equally well with worry or negative ideas. You can imagine countless things and sometimes they are charged by your emotions. Your thoughts can quite literally create any number of negative and positive outcomes around you.

Soon you will be able to make positive changes in your life simply and powerfully. A child can do this, but you have the advantage of greater experience and wisdom. I hope you will use the information here to bring your dreams to life.

This is true for everyone who picks up this book:

**You are worthy enough to ask, and smart and talented enough to create what you desire.**

I love this phrase because it sticks in the mind but I mean it kindly:

**I want you to have an unfair advantage.**

When I use the word manifesting, you may think of creating. To my ear, creating is a child making a drawing, a chef tweaking a recipe or an entrepreneur writing a business plan. Manifesting goes beyond creating. I use the term manifesting in the biggest possible sense. Like Moses parting the Red Sea, it implies a magical and majestic act of creation without pencil and paper, without hands-on manipulation and physical limits. For simplicity, I will use manifesting and creating interchangeably here. Create unlimited wonders: Manifest big!

**The act of creation is not a magician's trick, it is everyone's gift and easy to do. It is one of the keys to the universe for you to use.**

## Create the Good

Manifesting is invisible but powerful and it has been taught for a very long time in numerous ways. I can't tell you that I have the ultimate method, but I can offer you a routine and formula that simply works. Everything required to manifest successfully is here. Create the good and comfort you require in your life and remove your guilt, issues and obstacles. Manifest what is positive for you and leave the rest behind.

For years I've listened to a lot of people discuss and give advice on the best possible way to bring things into people's lives. People compiled texts, compared stories, methods and results. Common threads and best practices emerged, resulting in many books and lectures.

Over the years, manifesting became a common topic. I am very happy more people are creating good things in their lives by essentially following the old wisdom, "Ask and you shall receive."

In my case, I learned about manifesting directly, not from books, but in a very hands-on way from Judy Goodman, William Buhlman and others. I didn't have prior knowledge of manifesting and had no real instruction, manual or philosophy on the subject, but I was successful anyway.

This direct education showed me over and over that thought is a force. Thought happens in real-time and causes an effect immediately. I was clearly shown that manifesting is both an act of creation and attraction available to anyone. I learned to harness the power of thought in a unique way and I am passing it on to you.

But before we talk about all of that, here is a story about asking in its simplest form.

## Make a Wish

I always encourage people to ask…to make wishes. I am continually amazed by people who won't ask for themselves. They pray and petition for world peace, their children, immediate family, for rain and more, but not for them alone. Their unselfishness is commendable, but I firmly believe it is allowed and advantageous to sometimes ask for yourself.

I often feel compelled to ask people to make a wish, to make a lot of wishes. The request certainly gets a reaction since I don't look like their fairy godmother. When I see that blank look on their faces, I say, "You do ask for things don't you?" Many do, and our conversation follows along the lines of what was asked for and how it worked out. Those discussions are pretty upbeat.

For those who don't ask, the typical responses are along the lines of, "I used to ask, but my wishes and prayers happened. It scared me, so I stopped."

Or I hear, "I don't think I should be asking for myself. I don't deserve that."

Or "I never get around to doing it."

Sometimes people break down in tears. On occasion, I've had to grab a chair because a person's knees began to buckle. Perhaps they had been waiting for permission and the opportunity overwhelms them.

Do all of these people subsequently embrace the moment and begin asking? No, most do not. I like to check back from time to time and I find that less than half eventually do. Happily, I do get the occasional good story from the group that does.

**If you never turn another page in this book that's perfectly okay, but allow me this request: I want you to make some wishes. They are just for you, no one else.**

It just may be that asking gets better results than not asking at all. Why not give it a try?

Nobody's looking. Here's an example of someone who gave it a try with a striking result.

## Next-day Service

I met my friend John Horan many years ago through the Denver Hospice. He is the CEO and president of Horan & McConaty, a fifth-generation provider of mortuary services in the Denver area. John and his company have won many awards for their business practices and civic service. Let me also add that John is fun to hang around with. I never dreamed I would have a pal in the mortuary business.

One evening, the two of us were talking when the impulse hit me to suggest that John make a wish. "What about?" he asked.

I said that it was just for him. "Make more wishes if you like, but they are just for yourself," I said.

"I have everything I need," he replied. "I would wish for my family."

"Certainly, wish for your family if you like," I said, "But this is just for you."

He thought for moment. "What I really need is a business decision," he said. "We want to open another mortuary and we are trying to make a judgment on the best location. My board is leaning towards an older part of town and I'm thinking of going south into a newer area. This new facility represents a very big investment and I want to make the best possible decision."

It was a nice moment. "Go ahead and wish for that," I said.

The next afternoon, John called. He began with the magic words I often hear from people who are manifesting. "You're not going to believe what just happened! I was on an early flight and I was doing the zigzag in the airport security line when a man behind me read my luggage tag. He asked if I worked for Horan & McConaty and I told him I was the president."

The man told John he was part of a city planning team for Highlands Ranch, a large bedroom community south of Denver. The team had identified the need for a mortuary in Highlands Ranch and he had recommended John's company. He was delighted to suddenly meet John in person.

As the conversation went forward, John realized that the best location would be in the newer communities to the south.

Months later, a very nice location was secured and their beautiful facility was almost finished when I got another call from John. He wanted to buy a number of my artworks for his new facility and I cheerfully accepted his offer. It was a big thank you from John and happily, they liked the artworks in the new mortuary.

After about a year, John told me the new facility was a tremendous success, beyond their estimates. He couldn't thank me enough and wanted to do something else for me. I was happy with his success and said, "I really didn't have anything to do with this. You're the one who made the wish."

"But I want to," John said, "so here's what I'm going to do. You're going to get a free funeral service on the house."

Well that was a stunner! It just made me giggle. He assured me he wasn't kidding and I replied, "Wow, I'm the first one on my block to get a free sendoff!" What a profound and unique gift. I have to say that sometime back I did ask for something along the lines of a VIP ride into the afterlife. I think John's gift is a very good start.

John simply asked for something specific and the next day he was given precisely what he had wished. Anyone can make these requests. You're fully empowered, so give yourself permission to ask.

It doesn't matter what you think of yourself now. Be assured that you are more than powerful and capable enough, and it is my wish that you become very, very happy. Your joy may become contagious, bringing cheer to others. I hope it does.

I would gently offer: Please share your happiness modestly and considerately.

# TWO

## First Adventures:
## The Rose and a Duck

Once upon a time, a long, long time ago I was drowning with an issue in my life. (Who doesn't have a personal issue or few?) This was my serious, personal issue that I couldn't shake and didn't understand. It seemed beyond my ability to make a change or understand what was happening. I can still clearly remember going right to the top with a prayer. I followed my belief and asked God for help because I was very weak and failing. Amazingly, within a month I was thrown a life preserver. I had recently become acquainted with a writer in the metaphysical field and it occurred to me that she might know some intuitives (psychics) in the United States. I felt if I could understand the reason I was acting as I was, then perhaps I could solve my problem. Perhaps someone with greater insight could provide the answers I needed. My acquaintance gave me the phone number of a woman far more gifted than I could understand, Judy Goodman.

I was very nervous but I called Judy immediately and we instantly became close friends. We stayed in very close contact and she helped me immensely. Being mentored and befriended by Judy was an answered prayer. She is quite possibly the most gifted person in the western world. She has a number of gifts that allow her to see and communicate with those in spirit, retrieve hidden information and much more. Judy is very aware, accessing the seen and unseen worlds. Her sensitivity, access to information and clarity are remarkable. Throughout the years I have observed and worked closely with many extraordinarily gifted and intuitive people but none like Judy.

My personal issue was certainly helped by the information that Judy later provided, but my contact with her opened the door to an unexpected new world.

## The First Gift

I had been speaking with Judy for a few weeks when a kind woman, a stranger, called to ask me if I knew what Judy could really do. Judy had instructed this person to get in touch with me so I would better understand Judy's abilities. At the time, my relationship with Judy was like a client. We were becoming fast friends, but I really didn't know her well. I didn't understand what this call was about so I asked the caller to elaborate. She patiently explained to me some of Judy's many abilities. I clearly recall being familiar with many of the talents she described but completely baffled and surprised by some of Judy's other capabilities. The woman on the phone said that if I were to send Judy something in thought, she would get it. "Get what?" I asked. The caller replied, "She will be able to see your thought form up in spirit, not our physical world, but what is commonly called the other side."

The caller explained to me that she had sent Judy gifts in the past using her thoughts and that Judy clearly saw and described the thought that was sent. Keep in mind that you and I wouldn't see these thoughts in our physical world, but Judy could. Clearly, something besides a conjuror's trick was at work here.

Judy and I continued conversing more on the phone and became close friends. I was learning about spiritual matters and my head was swimming with the possibilities and vastness of it all.

Some weeks passed, and it was the eve of Judy's birthday. I called and asked if she would participate in a little experiment. I had decided to send her something in thought that day. She agreed and asked me, "So how are you going to do it?" I wasn't sure. My best plan was to concentrate really hard on what was to be her birthday gift and somehow get it to her. I had understood, and she had confirmed, that thought was tangible and instantaneous.

"Look, it's really simple," Judy said. "You're going to think of the thing in your mind and since it is a gift, it's going to come from your heart. Your thought is going to be very powerful that way. Just think of the object for a few seconds and let it go. Since it is a gift, this thought will come from your heart automatically and I'll get it every time." Judy also affirmed that it is not necessary to be creative or have visual talent. Anyone can imagine an object well enough and fine detail is not required.

Here's a personal note: I'm a guy who is not attentive enough to subtleties. A guy thing? Perhaps, but certainly something for me to work on. So you just read what Judy said about the heart, but all that I remembered was to think of the gift and send it. Heart? What heart?

I thanked her and got off the phone. "Wow," I thought to myself, "There may be something to this. She didn't say I was crazy and she approved of the whole idea."

The next day was Judy's birthday. It gave me butterflies to think of what I was about to attempt. There I was in San Francisco, planning to send a birthday present in thought to Columbus, Georgia, a place 2,400 miles away. I began thinking about what to send and an idea came to me quickly. I envisioned a yellow rose in a simple silver vase. I didn't need a photograph for reference, the object was easy to imagine. I held the idea for a few brief seconds and let it go as a gift to Judy. I didn't have any concerns about the impossibilities or the distances involved. I took a few seconds and effortlessly sent my gift in thought as if I had done it a hundred times.

Later, as I drove to work, I began having second thoughts. This couldn't be that easy, so I crammed and jammed that thought over and over again until lunchtime. I was making sure that she would get the yellow rose. I was using brute force, and a lot of it.

Work was close to my house, so I drove home for lunch and called Judy.

I was on pins and needles when I heard her pick up. "Did you get the thing I sent?" I asked.

"Hang on," she said. "I'm looking at the computer screen. Okay, I can clearly see all that is in the room. There are a lot of people on the other side who know it's my birthday today, so the room is filled with gifts from them." (Keep in mind that most of us wouldn't see these gifts because they appear only in the world of spirit. They would be invisible to us in the same way that ghosts are.) "There are also a lot of people in the physical world who are aware of my birthday and they have sent a lot of gifts as well," she continued. "Ken, your gift is right up front, here on the desk." I was so eager to know if she got my gift!

I'll never forget what happened next.

"Was it your intention to send me a rose?" she asked. My heart jumped into my throat, choking me a little. I couldn't believe that she got it. This was a Hollywood moment. "Yes!" I replied.

"Was it your intention to send me a yellow rose?" she continued. "Yes, yes it was!" I was so excited. This was unbelievable. How could something like this be happening? It was so simple but incredibly profound. I had really done it, but then Judy added, "Well, that's not what I got."

What? "What do you mean that's not what you got?" I felt the rug pulled out from under me. She saw the rose but that's not what she got?

I shot right back, "I don't understand what you mean."

A long teacher pause followed and then Judy continued, "Someone saw your intention, embellished it and then sent it on its way."

I was scrambling for solid ground. "I'm totally confused," I said. "We had talked about this. I understood that thought is instantaneous across any distance. There is no time lag. You think it and the thought arrives anywhere, instantly. Who could possibly grab my instantaneous thought, embellish it and then send it on its way?"

"Some big guy," Judy said.

"What do you mean, 'big guy?' " I couldn't believe this. I had already experienced an impossible development and now something even more improbable has been created by some invisible person.

"Some big guy," she repeated, "J.C."

"What? Jesus? J.C. big guy?" I said in complete disbelief. She confirmed it and I just hung there on the phone in silence. I couldn't wrap my arms around this. Jesus is a name I don't use very much. I'm really not the born-again, saved-again type, but I certainly feel a deep respect and awe for him. I keep his name in reserve, as well as God and all of the great religious figures. I'm not accustomed to having divine figures come up in conversation. Judy was aware of that and used his nickname on my behalf. "I don't understand Judy, what is it you're trying to say?"

She chose her words very carefully. "What I'm looking at is a rose that has been dipped in gold and is all aglow. I couldn't see the color of it because there's so much light coming from the now golden rose. I had to play 1-800 psychic; I had to guess. I had to intuit that you sent me a yellow rose.

"By the way," she added, "you did great, but I could tell you overworked it."

I was stunned. She clearly saw my intention but also how it had been embellished and by whom. I didn't know what to say, but I believed something real occurred. Someone had altered my simple gift, turning it into something far more profound.

We continued to talk for a time, but I can't remember a single word beyond the conversation I've described here. Those important moments were burned into my memory, nothing else. For days after, I considered that by simply using my thoughts, I sent a rose; it was held for a moment and then beautifully enhanced. Obviously, something big was going on, but what?

## Special Delivery

From time to time over the following year, I continued to send things in thought to Judy. It was like a game I played. Sometimes my thoughts were embellished and other times not at all. On one occasion, a group of my friends at lunch combined our intentions to send an autumnal bouquet to Judy. I immediately called her on behalf of the group and she accurately reported what we had intended. Judy described a large bouquet of plants in fall colors. The arrangement was large, very beautiful and with little sparks coming off of it. She got the gifts sent to her in thought every time. Note that Judy allowed this "connection" from the group and me on occasion and she was open to my sending her things. It was like a student given the phone number of the teacher. If that student calls, the teacher recognizes the caller and picks up, but not all of the other calls get through. Don't bother pestering Judy or your favorite target out of curiosity, it's unlikely the gifts will be seen or felt.

Now I'm not the brightest bulb in the box. Want the proof? For about a year, I had been shown with absolute certainty that thought was something real. So? I didn't do anything with it other than play with the concept. The staggering importance of this never dawned on me. What an impressive and empowering tool simple thought could be! One day all of that changed. It was about a year after the yellow rose event when this singular thought popped into my head.

I immediately called Judy. "Hey Judy, are you busy?"

"No," she said. "What's up?"

I told her I had an idea. "Just one?" she said jokingly.

Yeah, yeah… I told her about my idea to try out thought in a new way. I asked if she had a chair in front of her and yes, she did. "So here is the plan," I said. "I'm going to send you something in thought and put it into your chair. If you would, stay on the phone with me in real time while I do this. You can describe what is being manifested as it happens." She agreed and I began to think about what I would send with just my thoughts. Only Judy could see the object being sent, this is the only expectation I had. Never did I dream of making something physically appear. The importance here was to send thought to someone who could see it as it appears non-physically. What would that be like?

I got the idea that thought is material, but I didn't understand the mechanisms involved. I still don't really know, but I leaped in. It occurred to me that I should send something unique. It was also important to consider some unknowns. If kids were playing outside next to my house, would their thoughts get in the way of what I was trying to send to Judy? Would other thoughts floating around in the air interfere with what I was trying to do? To make a good proof, I definitely had to come up with a unique object, something that would not be floating around. So here's what I came up with: I would send Judy a 5-foot-tall Daffy Duck and place him in that chair. He would be holding a vertical stick about 3 feet tall and at the top a flat, horizontal board would be attached. Written on the front of the board in red lipstick would be the word love. Perfect! Surely no one else would be sitting around thinking about some duck holding a little handmade sign with a stick.

Remember when I sent the yellow rose? Judy said that since it was a gift, I would create the thought in my head and the idea would then flow out through my heart, the ideal combination. This business with the heart was a subtlety that I had completely forgotten. I was gearing up to send Daffy when Judy asked, "So how are you going to do this?"

I was ready. "I'm going to concentrate on this really hard and send it to you," I replied.

"Go for it, Bucko," Judy cracked. Bucko? Bucko? Grasshopper? She never called me Bucko. What's up with that? I didn't care, I was on a mission and I was going to make this happen guy-style and bludgeon that Daffy Duck into existence!

I began concentrating and visualizing Daffy Duck sitting in Judy's chair with his handmade sign. It was hard to sustain my vision. I wondered if people are truly able to focus on something like this. How do they keep their thoughts from sailing away to some other shiny horizon? This exercise was really important, but regardless, my mind quickly went to putty. Despite myself, I was able to patch together a pretty good effort and after two minutes I was worn out but ready.

"So," I asked Judy, "what do you see?"

I'll let that question just hang here for a moment.

# THREE

## Manifesting in Real Time: Thoughts and Lists

Here is what I knew about working with thought and manifesting at this point: About a year or so before this Daffy Duck moment, I became very close friends with William Buhlman. William is a best-selling author on the subject of out-of-body or astral traveling. I don't want to get too far afield here, but William and Judy had both shared with me their vast experiences and observations from visiting the other side. They are both adept at out-of-body travel. They can leave their physical bodies and using the etheric or spirit body that we all possess, travel in the spiritual or astral realms. Their level of consciousness is beyond even lucid dreaming. They are very awake and aware of their surroundings. Beyond this physical world there is a lot of territory. Earth is very small in comparison to all that there is beyond our physical world. It is a fascinating subject and they indulged my many questions. One of the topics I had discussed with my very experienced friends is how thought is manifested in the nonphysical world.

This is what I learned: Wishes, intentions and thoughts begin to form up on the other side like wisps of smoke. The more you think on them, the more "layers" of intention you give these thoughts, the more solid they become. These wisps of smoke then become more solid and begin to take on a three-dimensional shape. If you continue, the form takes on blushes of color, becomes more solid, and then it becomes fully colored and fully formed, all on the other side. At that point, your thought is quite complete and it will become more compatible with the physical world than the nonphysical world. Your fully formed thought will become physical and manifest itself here. You have made it so. This is so very, very simple but it takes a willingness and some effort on your part to complete the process of bringing the thought into reality.

William would make lists and vision boards of what he wanted in his life, and during his out-of-body travels, he would sometimes view how his thoughts were forming up on the other side. The items on his list could be a common object like a new roof or a concept like health. Judy could do this as well. So many times I asked William and Judy,

"You can really see your thoughts actually form up over there?" They assured me they could.

**Back to my question for Judy. "So, what do you see?"**

We had remained quietly on the phone together while I was trying to send the duck, so I wasn't prepared for her sudden and aggressive response. When I asked her what she saw, Judy answered in such an intimidating way I didn't have the space to think. Anything I had previously learned about how thought forms up was pushed to the side.

"You're just making smoke!" she observed. "Look, if you put out a wimpy thought you get a wimpy response. There is just smoke in the chair. If you want to really make something, you have to really get on this! You have to really try and make this happen!"

I had never heard her speak to me this way. I was stunned. I was failing and wasting her time. I was doing a pitiful job and completely embarrassing myself...a wimpy job!

Suddenly I was re-energized. I pushed and pushed that Daffy Duck with his handmade sign for another four minutes. If I thought I was worn out from concentrating before, I was totally exhausted after my second attempt.

"I'm just cooked and I don't have anything left. I don't know what else to do, Judy, so what do you see?" I asked hopefully. This was a very important moment for me and I remember her response very clearly.

"Was it your intention to send me a cartoon character?" she teased.

This was another of those Hollywood moments. "Yes!" I said in a state of wonder and shock.

"Well," Judy continued, "what I'm looking at is some 2½-foot-tall, poor human-ey thing. It's got little skinny arms and legs with cartoon colors on it, so I figured it's a cartoon character and it's got a stick in its hand."

What an amazing moment! I fell back into the chair victorious! It was absolutely amazing! I yakked on and on and laughed like a kid. I was so very happy and in such wonder at what had transpired.

Through Judy's patience and coaching, she had given me something very important. My thoughts could create a fairly complicated form out of thin air almost instantly. I was convinced that I didn't perform as well as possible or as efficiently, but it did manifest in a shape very close to my design. Wow!

Only later did I realize I had begun to make smoke in the chair just as William and Judy had described it to me. My thought had begun to appear as form! I was a smoke-making, Daffy Ducking son of a gun! Judy's assertive response really jolted me and pushed me harder to a successful result. I also realized that anybody could do this if they wanted to. Later, you will learn an elegant and simple method to use your thought as a tool. High levels of concentration and brute force will not be necessary.

So what did I do with this hard-earned knowledge? Um, nothing much.

## Making a List

Using thought in real-time to make something in spirit was a great experience and I told my friends about it. I possessed this interesting knowledge, but never made the connection to use it in a practical way. I had this profound experience with Judy and I knew William was making lists successfully, but these were two different experiences to me. I observed that thought was instantaneous in the non-physical world and the lists and vision boards took time to become physical. I wasn't much on making lists at that time, it just didn't sing to me. Sending things to Judy was fun and very intriguing, but I just didn't associate it to any sensible purpose. I didn't see that these two activities were essentially the same and incredibly useful.

Shortly after my experience with sending thought, The Secret, a movie expressively about manifesting, came out. I watched it a number of times and shared it with friends. I really understood the film's message because I was in that choir. I had witnessed manifesting, sending things to Judy via thought numerous times. My friend William was making his personal wish lists and they were coming true. After the items on William's first list came to fruition, William called me to say he was starting a second list. The first item was not just visiting China, but being in China for an extended length of time. In a matter of weeks, he called me back and told me that his wife, a manager for General Motors, had been offered a job with an extended residency in China. Off they went, for years! Their results were hard to believe but I was encouraged and became a list maker myself.

I would make a written list of things and concepts to manifest. Some of my items listed for improvement included income, my painting career and a relationship. I would also make a vision board by covering a large sheet of paper or poster board with photographs of items and concepts I wanted to bring into my life. With a vision board, you can picture that wonderful vacation, the college degree and that sweet red car. You can also illustrate concepts. Your blissful relationship may be a picture of a radiant couple. You new joy is represented by the girl happily jumping to reach the sky.

I had learned to strengthen my thought by adding more layers of intention to my list and vision board. The concept is to add more and more layers of intention until your thought becomes physical. In the non-physical world you are making your thoughts start as smoke then take on more and more form. You keep layering your intentions until they successfully emerge into your physical environment.

To add more intention and power to my written list, I would start with a very special piece of paper, not copy paper, but stationery purchased just for this occasion. Then I would go out of my way to find a writing instrument and envelope in another room. I wouldn't use materials nearby. Each time I went out of my way to manufacture this list, the intention was reaffirmed and increased.

I would date the paper and then make my list. Once it was made, I stamped the envelope and mailed it to myself. Since this represented an opportunity to add another layer to my intentions, I would drive out of my way to post it in a mailbox far from my house. Every physical action increases the power of the thought.

Once my list came back to me in the mail, I would place it on the counter and burn a candle over it or put it under my pillow at night. I was adding physical effort and emotion with these small rites. All these acts would increase the power of my thought layer upon layer, day after day. Months later, I would open my envelope and see how I was doing. I was getting results. Most of the hopeful intentions I wrote down came true. Most items would be common to anyone's list but in some cases I was targeting more unique concepts and they were appearing in my life. There was something to this manifesting.

## The Vision Board

Sometimes my vision boards are singularly tasked. At one point, I owned two homes and it was putting me in a big financial bind. When I put one of the houses on the market, I created a vision board covered with photos of the home. I placed my "house for sale" vision board in my closet so I would see it every morning when I dressed and in the evening before bed. If I was around during the day, I often displayed it in whatever room I occupied.

The housing market was terrible. The recent recession was in full swing and few if any houses in the neighborhood were selling. I tried another tactic by writing on my board, "This house will sell for a profit." A few more months went by and this vision board was beginning to smell like a flop. A part of me was feeling desperate, but I knew I had to stay on a positive track. In a practical and creative moment, I crossed out the word profit and replaced it with "at a price I'm very happy with." That did the trick! Within a few weeks, I had a clean, firm offer that I was very happy to accept. I had one of the few sales during that period at a reasonable price. I was very, very grateful. Later in this guide we are going to take these concepts of manifesting even further.

I began to notice numerous books and videos on manifesting techniques. It had become a very popular topic. Personally, I was doing pretty well with my efforts. Occasionally there were quick results, some results took many months and others didn't seem to happen at all. The bottom line was that the people I knew who were really working with manifesting on a steady basis were happy with their progress. They were asking, praying, listing, vision boarding, you name it. People were taking action and getting more results than they had previously.

I was struck by all of their "before" stories of lack and need. Even more, I was surprised by the large number of people reluctant to ask, to request things for themselves. So many kind people would pray to directly help others, but they wouldn't do the same for themselves. These considerate individuals would rarely make requests on their own behalf. Fortunately, as the idea of manifesting grew in the public mind, more people began to give it a try.

People were proactively creating. Instead of waiting for something to come their way or sitting back and hoping for the best, many were now using everything at their disposal to create positive change. They wanted better careers, travel opportunities, good relationships, financial security and more.

**More people understood they could have more fulfillment and comfort in their lives.**

Of those who wanted change and were intrigued by the list and vision board information, only a fraction of them stayed with it. In a large number of cases I noticed that many were tripping over some of the concept "requirements." Many had the impression that they weren't doing something right or that they were not adept at what was asked of them. Often the entire manifesting idea wasn't really that appealing or believable. For others, they felt they weren't consistent or were lacking some intangible something to be successful.

Then I came across an idea that changed everything. It was genius.

# FOUR

## Manifesting #1:
## A Key to the Kingdom

**What is the difference between a big miracle and a little one? Nothing.**

For many generations, numerous people have expressed the idea that thought is not an abstraction, but something tangible. Positive thinking and actions, prayer and meditation are commonly attributed to improving lives. Negativity and fear are said to produce the opposite effect. I ascribe to those philosophies and thought is at the core.

Stacks of books have offered the idea of thought being a tool, something to build with, a way the mind can influence reality. Most of the manifesting teachings are the result of accumulated experiences. People try out different approaches to manifesting and they compare their results. Over time, these compilations of shared experiences lead to the best strategies for maximum results.

I followed the literature, but I never really experienced thought as a reality until I was sending things directly to Judy. I didn't have a formula or guide to the best practices. I simply sent a thought with the clear intention to create something, but I had no idea what I was doing.

**It didn't matter what I didn't know or what I may have lacked, thought happened anyway and it will do the same for you.**

Sure, my vision boards and lists were doing pretty well, but it seemed fanciful and indirect. It was my hopeful exercise, but at the time I didn't KNOW if progress was being made. I was in the waiting game. I would send up prayers, make lists, boards and hope something was going on over there. Doubts appeared: I'm not doing it right… If only I were a better person… I'm not deserving. Am I being punished? Is God just too busy? Does God exist? God? God?

I had doubts like everyone else. I had experienced thought not as a concept but as something real and repeatable. If I sent something in thought to Judy, she got it every time. But incredibly, I still didn't link my direct experiences with Judy to what was occurring with my lists or vision boards.

At the heart of this experience I knew that thought is real. It is as effective as pushing an elevator button. The elevator starts to move toward you. Sometimes it comes quickly; sometimes it has to move a longer distance to eventually reach you. No matter, it's coming towards you because you pushed the button.

## Thought as Natural Law

Put your hand in front of a light source. It will make a shadow every time because it is fundamental to the way light works. Put your hand over a burning match and you will quickly feel the heat. It is fundamental to the way heat works. Look at your tabletop. Everything is resting on the table, nothing is floating away. Because of what? Gravity. Heat, light and gravity operate according to real, natural laws and thought is real as well. Thought creates and that is fundamental to the way thought works.

When you are dealing with the fundamental laws of nature, it doesn't matter if you understand how these laws work. The laws don't care if you understand the physics. Gravity, light, thought and other natural laws do not differentiate between a terrible person and a saint. It doesn't matter what you believe or comprehend about these laws, they just work anyway. The fundamental laws of nature do not judge.

**Thought is real. Use it.**

A hammer is real; you can drive nails with it. A car is real; you can drive places with it.

Thoughts are real and they create things in unlimited ways.

When you are manifesting, you are in essence making a mold. With this shape you fashion something incredible, something powerful. By using ceremony, concentration or repetition, you begin to fill the mold, making your thoughts manifest. Add the emotional power of love or fear and the mold begins to fill with the equivalent of quick-set concrete. You can create the things you love or what you fear. What do you want to create for yourself?

**What can you do with unlimited thought?**

Here's an example—and forgive me in advance for making it a little harsh—but it is a powerful and purposely memorable statement.

One September morning in 1939, Adolf Hitler woke up and declared, "I'm going to invade Poland today." He did and 100,000 angels did not stop his army at the Polish border. It was allowed. The invasion was a great tragedy for the world, but it was allowed.

This is the Wild Wild West here in the physical world. Anything can be made possible if you can think it: good things and horrible things.

Look around your house. Everything that is non-organic in your home was a thought before it was made physical. Take a paperclip, a button, a sheet of paper, then consider the thousands of man-hours that brought that object into being. A paperclip was mined as ore from the earth, smelted and then formed, packaged, distributed, advertised and offered for sale to you. The paperclip and all the other things in your home began first as a thought.

**Thoughts can manifest objects or concepts.**

A few months back, William and I were having a lunch in an idyllic, country club setting. It was a perfect day with picturesque houses, manicured lawns and small, puffy clouds in a blue sky. We were talking about manifesting and how thought appears on the other side. We were discussing how things form up from smoke first and then congeal into a recognizable object. In the non-physical realm, cars and other objects form up to eventually look like the item the thinker intended. "What about concepts like joy or success?" I asked. William pointed to the perfectly formed clouds in the sky and said, "They look like those small clouds. The concept you create begins as a wisp and then becomes a very well-defined cloud. When you view something like that cloud over there, you understand what that cloud represents. You can see how the concept is evolving by how well the cloud is defined."

**Again: What can you do with unlimited thought? Better still, what is the most effective way to use this amazing tool?**

So, let's think, "Thought can do anything, thought can do anything.... but what, what, what is the best way to use it? What is the most efficient way to create your desires?"

What you'll read next is one of the keys to the kingdom.

## Buy Your Ticket

We can all imagine something that we want to happen. When you plan a vacation you have expectations. You imagine the beach chair, the view or the marvelous walks. We can imagine pleasant things or conceive negative outcomes. Either way, your thoughts begin to make that smoke on the other side. Stay with it and your thought begins to take form. Make that Daffy Duck if you like, but let's do something really, really big, just for you. Here is a concept that has been expressed in different ways and at different times for years, but this valuable concept is usually not mentioned or stressed enough. It is pure genius and now it is yours.

**Close your eyes, and imagine that you are in your future.**

Thought will do anything, including creating your future. By imagining that you are in your future, you are efficiently using thought in a very powerful way. Consider traveling by bus to a favorite city? Wonderful, but don't buy a bus ticket and imagine sitting on the bus with endless stops before you get there. Buy your ticket and be instantly where you want to be!

Don't get on board and consider everything that has to happen before you arrive. Why? Because your thoughts will require you to make every little stop on the way. Instead of being in your future, you'll be traveling as your thoughts instructed, poking along, visiting every little dot on the map. Your thoughts have required that A has to follow B, and so on. It doesn't matter how you get to your destination, you just will because your thoughts can create your future.

**The most efficient way to get to where you're going is to imagine that you're in your future and create your future from there.**

If you think it up, the image begins to form on the other side as what looks like smoke. Thought can create the now and it can create the future. Let's be smart and go for the future!

The key to manifesting this way is for you to stay with it and build the smoke into a form that becomes more and more solid. Carry on and it becomes more substantial, eventually taking on a blush of color. When you continue with your intention, your thought becomes even more solid, eventually going full-color, then becoming 3-D and completely formed. At that point your thought comes over, manifesting into the physical world. Your thought has become real. This is fundamental to the way thought works. Want to create heat? Keep rubbing sticks together. Want to make thought real? Reinforce the thought until it comes into the physical world.

When I was sending things to Judy I used brute force. It required a lot of concentration on my part and don't forget; only she could see them. I never made my thought physical, but I learned how thought begins to form and that thought definitely creates.

So far, so good. If you stay with your thoughts, they will eventually make something, but there is much more. Here is a powerful and singularly efficient way to increase the power of your thoughts. It's easy to access, but I lost it in the subtlety way back when I first started sending thoughts to Judy. Before I sent her the rose, she instructed me to just think of the object and since it's a gift to her, my intention will automatically go out through my heart to her. So what was Judy trying to tell me? Simply put, she wanted me to use the power of love to increase the strength of my intention. In guy-speak, when you use love, you engage the afterburners.

## Pick a Side

Here is a common wisdom:

**There are two things in this world: love and fear.**

Both are extremely strong forces and when you consider it, you see them everywhere. So when I sent Judy the rose as a gift, it was a loving gesture. Remember what she said? "...it will come from your heart and I will get it every time." That's what happens when you marry your intention with love.

We are surrounded in a field of unfocused energy: love and fear, positive and negative. There are times in our lives when our love is focused. When we fall in love or have children, it is quite clear we are loving in a very intense way. Fear can be focused as well. We have all experienced terror, anxiety and debilitating worry. This is fear focused.

It's your option to pick a side, love or fear. What do you want to create for yourself? With the techniques offered here, you can learn to use the positive force to shape your life and diminish the effects of fear and its negative influence.

Let's put it all together and create a template for using thought in the most powerful and streamlined way. First, I'd like you to finish the two-part statement below. You will imagine that you're in your future and you specify what you see, then you'll express how grateful you are. Your gratefulness is an expression of love. Here's the statement:

**I am in my future, and in my future** _____
_____.

Then allow yourself to feel and say, **"I am so very grateful."**

This exercise is what I call the Movie.

# FIVE

## In Your Movie:
## Your Future Scripted and
## Directed by You

When I envision my future, I refer to it as my Movie. I have a lot of different scenes in my very own Movie and in each one I am in my future, walking around, observing, touching and feeling. I really am grateful to be there because each scene is just as happy and perfect as I can imagine it. These scenes in my future are not about to happen, they have already happened!

**I don't think about how these scenes could possibly occur.**

Try it: Imagine you are walking around in one of your future scenes and all is amazingly pleasant. The problems you had no longer exist. You are living happily and comfortably. You have miraculously arrived. How did this happen? Standing in your future, you don't know, but it has happened. Don't consider how everything came about because it will limit your creation. Get the ticket to your destination and forget all the stops—just be there.

Remember, it doesn't matter how you got there, you're simply grateful to have arrived. You're creating your future only, not the myriad details that made it possible. If you're smart, you will leave the details alone. You are empowered to create your present or your future. It is allowed. Use what you are freely given and create the best life you can imagine in a future of your making. Go forth. Wash, rinse and repeat.

## It's Your Choice

When you go to a restaurant you have to give the waiter your order. When you are shopping, you pick up the things you came for or those items that catch your eye. In general, you don't count on the waiter to bring you your favorite dish or the store clerk to know what you need at home.

Eating out and shopping involve making relatively small decisions. When it comes to the BIG ONE, your own life, it is very important to know what you require. If you don't know, the default result is that you will do what someone else thinks you should do or end up with something that someone else thinks you should want. That someone else will make assumptions about what is important to you. They may impose limits that are not helpful. You may end up in the job your dad wants you to have or you may marry the woman your mom thinks is best for you. (Out of respect for all those moms and dads, they are absolutely correct in those areas at times... Just sayin'!)

**You are in a sea of other people's intentions.**

There are a lot of well-meaning people around you with ideas about what is best for you and far greater numbers surround you with their own intentions. It's up to you to decide and envision where your path will take you.

Let's "proof" it out with this example:

Imagine you are going to a museum downtown. You are driving on the interstate at 60 miles an hour. You have at least one hand on the wheel and you are pointing yourself to the museum's address. At times the traffic slows down and you may even encounter a detour, but you are continuously driving to the museum. No matter what comes on the radio or what the billboards say, you will continue to your destination. You know where you are going.

All is well, the traffic is flowing fine and you are making good time. There are 20 cars in view around you, all in the flow with each going to a different place.

**Now take your hands off the wheel.**

What happens next? Chaos. It will be like bumper cars and you will find yourself knocked right off the road. You have surrendered the responsibility of where you are going, and instantly you are without direction, swarmed by the intentions of others. It is as if you don't care, won't pay attention or you just relinquish your final outcome to others. It's very unlikely you are going to reach your destination this way. Your next ride may be in an ambulance. Being aimless on the highway is not a good practice!

Even though you can't see them, your intentions are very powerful. They are leading you on that path to your destination. There are countless stories of very successful and happy people who share a common wisdom. By whatever methods, they are using their actions, intentions, wishes, prayers, etc. to make good things happen. These people know where they are going. Perhaps you should, too.

I certainly don't have a final, ultimate method for bringing desired things into your life. But many have told me and I have witnessed in my own life, that this method of going into your Movie is amazingly simple and effective. Special skills, abilities or large amounts of time are not a requirement.

## Creating Your Future

Remember those questions I asked in the Introduction?

**What would you like to have in your life?**

**How would you script your life if you had the chance?**

**What are your wishes?**

**Do you long for better?**

Take some time now to answer those questions. With your answers in mind, you can begin producing your Movie.

**Be still and imagine you are in your future.**

This future is not currently unfolding or about to happen. You are in your future and this future has been in place for some time. Touch it, walk around in it, view it. You can imagine in high detail or you may opt not to visualize much at all. Regardless, it is your perfect scenario.

**When you are in your lovely future, say what you are grateful for or words to that effect.**

Remember that your thought is strong and by adding gratefulness or love, you are greatly magnifying your creation.

**Create your best possible scenario.**

A bit later in this chapter I'll give you some possible suggestions. You may have a scene for your career, your home, your finances, a relationship, etc. Include as much or as little detail as you'd like. Remember to express gratitude for what you see, hear and feel in your Movie. Involve all the senses you wish.

Being in your Movie once a day will be more than enough. You may find some days flow better than others, but don't judge yourself or the experience. You are definitely creating good things from your thoughts and heart, steadily, every day. If I were to recommend that you do your Movie three times a day you might think that replaying it 10 times a day is better. But we can't stay inside all day waiting for the future to happen. Once a day will do just fine.

I don't want to make running your Movie only once a day a hard and fast rule. After all, we're trying to make layers of intention, but don't get out of control. Occasionally I'll have a moment and I'll imagine I'm in my future at that very instant. For example, I might be driving and imagining that I'm going to my perfect home at that moment. It feels pretty good and I'll say I'm very grateful. I could be working and say that I'm in my future right now and in this future my perfect car is parked outside. I'm so grateful the car is not a financial burden and my perfect partner helped me pick it out!

Enjoy creating all the scenes in your Movie and spending brief amounts of time in each one. Your success is up to your imagination and heart. When that dream comes true you will likely share it with someone. I receive many happy calls that begin something like this, "You're not going to believe what just happened!" The callers are very excited. Me, too! I drop everything, sit down and listen. When they start to describe their story, the pure joy makes us both silly. We start shrieking at each other like teenage girls. "No way! That's impossible! Shut up! That can't happen!" How amazing to share news like that. Manifesting works and it gives us all hope for the future.

Bottom line: Do your Movie every day with all of your future scenes in it. In this way your future will have a nice flow and all of your senses will easily travel from scene to scene. Don't get distracted by trying to plug in bits and pieces of your future throughout the day. Set aside that one time to be completely in your future, then open your eyes and get back into your regular day. Don't neglect your day job, and be assured you are moving toward the future you're creating.

**Next, don't get in the way of your beautiful creation.**

## Helpful Hints

### *What is necessary?*

When I was learning to manifest, I didn't have any skill set or theory. I wasn't limited by a check list. I was told that manifesting was possible so I went for it. I had all the finesse of a child, but I got results.

A lot of alternate methods were certainly available. Teachers offered many paths such as prayer, positive thinking, meditation and more. Regardless of the method, many people were tripping up on the approaches required for success. They were not good at what they were being shown to do. Many people felt less than 100% capable and therefore they would get less than a 100% result.

My goal is to offer you something that's easy to grasp. You won't have to master complicated practices to be a success at manifesting this way. It is not a prerequisite to first examine your life and clear a list of self-improvement bullet points. Some of the concepts mentioned here keep people from trying manifesting in the first place. We have a tendency to judge or grade how we are doing. How often do we give ourselves an A+ in something? These judgments can affect our outcome in a negative way or even keep us from trying. The following hints are for opening doors and avoiding the limits.

### Do I need meditation skills?

I really don't meditate well and that's true for many people. Our minds tend to wander more than is optimal. Personally, I often go to sleep while meditating and even forget what I was thinking just seconds ago. I would get a very poor grade in meditation. It is a helpful skill, but not required for your success with manifesting here. The Movie is a form of meditation, but don't trip up on the term. Your way of doing the Movie is the right way.

### Do I have to be an upbeat and positive person?

It doesn't hurt, but keep in mind that gravity is not affected by the kind of day you are having, thank goodness! We are dealing with a universal law here. One of the earliest results from my Movie is that I felt happier. My friends were coming to me and saying, "So what's up with you?" I'm a pretty upbeat person, but my friends noticed that I was much "chirpier" than usual. I've found that being in my Movie actually makes me a bit more upbeat. I look forward to being in my future. Yes, be more positive in your day and meet your future halfway, but don't judge yourself harshly when you are not.

### What actions should I take?

If you're imagining a wonderful future where you are happy and whole, make the effort to be happy and whole now as well. If you desire to lose weight, then endeavor to start now. The weight you target is in your future, but don't expect this result to happen without some effort on your part. If it were my future, I would imagine that I'm at my ideal weight. I would also add that I'm very grateful at how smoothly the weight loss came about. I don't want to manifest a severe illness to drop those pounds.

### Do I have to believe in this process?

Haven't you witnessed things that were "outside the box?" Those impossible events are a part of your life. Your beliefs, or what you think you know, form the boundaries of your experience. What you believe also creates limits in your life. Please don't decide in advance what is impossible. You have experienced the unimaginable often and sometimes to your great delight.

Believing that thought is real may be incomprehensible for some. It is perfectly normal to think manifesting from thin air is impossible. But, it doesn't matter what you believe thought can do. Thought works anyway. Water running downhill is not waiting for your beliefs to kick in or for your permission to flow.

### What about faith?

How much belief and faith is required? Well, nothing is required.

Here's the operative phrase again: it doesn't matter if you "get it," or have a certain level of faith. Your thoughts and your future will naturally form as you observe them. They will become more solid and real each time you revisit them, regardless of your confidence to manifest them. If you think this works or you have some degree of faith about the process, then it will be helpful to the process—they are positive thoughts—but faith is not essential.

***What if I am religious or not religious, a believer of something, or completely skeptical, does that make a difference?***
I'm a believer in the power of prayer, and I believe in God. That's just me. I do pray and I also get into my Movie every day. That makes me a doubly careful person, a belt and suspenders type.

We all hold a lot of beliefs to be true. We have a pretty good perception of our surroundings and how they all hold together. We are comfortable in the framework we subscribe to.

All of us are continually exposed to new ideas and doctrines, rejecting some and keeping those that are agreeable to us. It is impossible to empirically prove all these concepts as true but we keep what is plausible or proven to be correct.

Our beliefs are thoughts and so our beliefs create. Your view can construct unlimited possibilities or severe limits in your life. Note that you will be less successful in manifesting something that is directly opposed to your beliefs. One thought is working against the other.

If you are highly opposed to the processes described in this book, then your chances of success are reduced. Perhaps you are a skeptic but open to convincing results. Good, you might want to simply give it a try and observe the results. After all, what have you got to lose? Give yourself the opening to say, "This is something I really know nothing about."

Think of manifesting here as a new novel recommended by a friend. She liked the book so much she wouldn't spoil it by revealing any part of the narrative. Your friend is hoping you will enjoy the story as much as she did. She was thrilled by the experience of something unexpected and rewarding so she chose to share it with you.

Hold up a glass of water and let it go. Unless you're in orbit, the glass will drop to the floor every time. Gravity is the law and so is thought. Thought is unlimited. It is not restrained by anyone's beliefs, religion or skepticism.

### *I'm not worthy.*

This sneaky phrase has stopped a thousand beginnings and aided countless failures. It has been used as an excuse to never try or ask for more. Surely in your heart you know better or require better. Your worthiness is really up to you, but here's some good news: It doesn't matter if you are worthy or what you think of yourself. Electricity works for you just as well as the folks down the street. The gravity you experience is not proportional to your perceived worthiness. You are the recipient of all that natural law allows, so create without judging yourself or your outcome in advance.

Thoughts are absolutely real. The way thought becomes may be

God answering every intention and prayer. Perhaps the He or She in charge just turns it over to angels or some kind of special box, automatically turning thought into matter. Maybe there is no God at all and some quirk of nature manufactures thoughts into objects and concepts. We can speculate all we want, but it doesn't matter anyway. Your intentions begin forming immediately and they are not judged as right or wrong. Everyone is worthy—including you.

**The Movie is something that anyone can do perfectly well.**

Even a child can watch a movie. Special expertise is not required. You don't go to a movie and say to yourself, "I got a D in watching that movie," or "I got a B+ in attending the show." Everyone is a natural at sitting in a theater, relaxed and watching the film. So enjoy your show and create good cinema for yourself.

If you miss a day, it's OK. Don't criticize or judge yourself, just get back into your Movie when you can. When I forget to do my Movie, it's as if a little bird is circling around saying, "Ken, do your Movie. It's the most important thing you can do today!" I have to agree. A large number of us have experienced too many miracles to stop now.

When I think of all the marvelous things I have dreamed up and brought into my life, I am convinced. Each day I go into my Movie and joyfully put the time in. I have observed that my Movie has often delivered results faster and brought me more success than my 40-hour work week could provide. Just working hard wouldn't produce all the over-the-top events I've been privileged to experience. I created a script and got results. I love the successful stories people bring to me and they are sprinkled throughout this book.

**Get out more. Say yes more.**

In your future all is well, but how did you get there? It's unlikely it all came in via FedEx. You probably made and received some very good breaks along the way. Once you start manifesting your good future you become the target of those good results, so do your part. Get out of the bathrobe and get back into your normal day. Accept more invitations. Have people over. Be available and increase the odds of your future finding you! Say yes more. Those invitations and calls may be your future knocking on the door. Your future is forming up and working to put you in it. The more you are moving around and connecting, the more opportunities your scripted future has to find you.

**Your Movie is the shortcut, the quickest way to get where you decide to go.**

The Movie is one of the greatest tools available to you. If you are having problems in your life, eliminate them from your future. The problem doesn't exist there! You prefer to see yourself in a better place or position in your life? Put it into your Movie!

Your thoughts are working in an unlimited field of possibilities.

Don't accept your present state. Why would you want to bring your baggage, uncertainties and unhappiness into your wonderful future? Plan to move forward. Escape! In your future you have eliminated the negativity. It doesn't matter how the problems disappeared, in your future they are nowhere to be seen or felt.

## Taste, Smell and Feel

You're in your future and you see what is around you, but looking is not all you can do. Each of your senses is another tool for creating your future. Should you imagine a seaside resort, walk around and sit in the furniture, go over to the window and open it. Listen to the birds, smell and breathe in the salty air. Bring in the details and don't forget to make sure you are in the scene. Creating these scenes is not a sophisticated exercise. You don't have to have an original or visual mind at all. You are the star of show!

Your emotions are even more powerful. Yes, create your scene first, but be sure to permit yourself to react and feel in your Movie as well. The emotions you feel are extremely important, a creative force. So when you allow an emotional response to what you're experiencing, you have magnified your creative ability exponentially. When you're walking around in your wonderful future, do what comes naturally, be thrilled, be grateful. This is manifesting in the simplest and most powerful form. A child can do this.

Your mind may wander; you might not get all the details, but don't be frustrated or concerned. Try to fully experience what you can, don't worry about perfect and that will be more than enough. Next, be grateful and go to the next scene. Tomorrow is another day and you will be back in your lovely future to experience it all again.

We all like the perfect outcome. What could be better? Let's make our future as perfect as possible. If you want to specify the seaside resort as a perfect destination, then use detail and all your senses including emotion to make it so. Sometimes it's best to leave the details out of your Movie. If you are looking for a wonderful companion, go for perfect by not using a visual of who this ideal person will be. In that way you won't limit all of the possibilities for your perfect partner. Does he absolutely have to be 6 feet tall? Why does she absolutely have to be a redhead? You will surely know perfect when you encounter The One in real life.

In some of my scenes I have intentionally set it up with nothing to see in that future moment. I like to use the device of observing results at the end of my day there. In this future I'm sitting on the couch in my perfect home and I observe that I have perfect health. I can also make the observation that I'm doing what I'm here to do and I'm grateful. I don't see any of these scenarios, I simply notice they have been happily been in place for some time. It's a way of taking an abstract concept or emotion and placing it into my future without a limiting or complicated visual. Did you notice that I added an element to that statement? I made sure that I was in my perfect house and that I felt grateful. Perhaps you will visualize your perfect health while on a vacation somewhere in the world.

## Sample Script

When I'm doing my personal Movie, I tend to concentrate on three basic themes.

**First, I prefer health. It is an obvious priority.**
**Second, I feel urged to do what I am here to do so I script it into my future.**
**The rest of the scenes are all about my living comfortably, my third focus.**

So the script for my Movie goes something like this:

**"I'm in my future and I have perfect health, physically, mentally, emotionally and spiritually."** (Just saying perfect health should do just fine, but I go for more.) This scene is easy for me to visualize. Since I'm in my future and I'm sitting on my couch at the end of the day. I simply observe that I've had perfect health for a long time. Then I say, "I am so grateful."

**"I'm in my future and I'm doing what I am here to do and I am so grateful."** I truly don't know what my calling is, but there are the recurring themes of being in service and helpful in my life. Doing what you are here to do could cover a wide range of vocations: parenting, being a good spouse, doing your job or volunteering. Perhaps what you are here to do can manifest itself within your career, a very fulfilling result. A parent is certainly about helping and supporting his or her children. A businessperson is at a minimum providing for himself, employees and clients. It's my hope that some of you will see your life unfolding in a new and more fulfilling way. When I'm doing what I'm here to do, it fills my cup as little else can so I have made it a priority.

**"I'm in my future, in my perfect home and I am so grateful."** Home is my base, where I begin and end the day. I like the stability of having a place to call home. As it turns out, my home is also a place I share with others who come to teach, write, gather and rest. My home gets a workout and it is a comfort for many. When I was manifesting my perfect home, I was careful not to visualize it in too much detail. You can bring in all the specifics you wish, but my approach was to find the perfect home without limits. I only imagined that this home had good natural light and high ceilings. I started imagining the kitchen, but let that thought go. I realized I was severely limiting the possibilities of my perfect home. Again, use all of the detail you want. In my case, I was willing to go for perfect with only a few specifics.

To manifest this idea, I simply imagined that I was sitting on my couch in my perfect home. In order to magnify my intention, I wanted to physically make contact with the home of my future. So I breathed in the air and rubbed the cushion of the sofa in my present home. Every day for months, I rubbed that sofa like Aladdin's lamp! The couch I owned would go into whatever house I would create, so the air and that couch became my physical contact to my perfect home of the future.

Through a series of extraordinary events, all unforeseen and seemingly impossible, I finally came to live in the perfect home I am in today. I have so many to thank and I am so very grateful. It is the home I envisioned with the good natural light and tall ceilings. The financial calculus favored me in unexpected ways. This house was on the market for a couple of years. No one wanted to live in it but me. When all was ready, I contacted a number of mortgage brokers to try to get approved to buy my present home. All of the brokers fell away except for two, and only one broker could get me the standard loan I needed. She stayed with me and worked for 90 days to find a bank that would approve my loan. Miraculously, it was approved with standard terms and with a well-known, reliable bank.

Many times a month I hug the walls of my perfect home. I am living in the impossible. My home is proof of concept. Thought manifests, thought is real and it can be used to good effect in our lives.

I could delete the scene of my perfect home now that I live here, but I leave it in my Movie. I continue to reinforce the idea that I'm living here and that I will continue to do so.

**"I'm in my future, in my art studio and I am doing a lot of wonderful, new artworks. I am very successful and I am so very grateful."** As an artist, it is important for me to be successful in my career. In this scene, I spend a bit of time in the studio and I can see a lot of finished works that just thrill me. But all I really see are whitish canvases on the easels. They are great, new works but I don't want to see what they look like. I don't want to limit the finished product. In the

Movie, I specify that I get better with each new work. The paintings are exciting and of course, they are very successful in the marketplace. I also note that in my future, these new works are created in a very efficient way so that I am struggling less and painting better. It is great to be in my future specifying success without limits or detail.

Everything that I put in my art scene has come to pass. I've expanded this original concept of that script with even better results and I am very grateful.

Last year, my good friend and fellow artist Cheryl St. John and I had art openings across the street from each other in Taos, New Mexico. We had a little time together and talked about manifesting as a way to bring good things into our lives, art careers included. Every day after that discussion, Cheryl used the manifesting methods discussed here. Weeks later, she entered a juried contest, the 2012 Capitol Christmas Tree Art Competition. As a prestigious competition with high visibility, this event attracts a lot of artists from around the country.

Cheryl received great news: She won first place! There was a handsome cash prize and more. She was flown to Washington D.C. for the Christmas tree lighting ceremony and was part of a presentation program that included the speaker of the U.S. House of Representatives. It was a whirlwind few days and she had quite the story to tell when she got back. Cheryl was using manifesting in an unlimited way to further her career and she got fantastic results.

Last night I saw Cheryl again at another of her gallery openings. She was recently selected for representation by one of the best and most established galleries in Denver. She let me know she was still in her Movie, happily manifesting every day.

**"I'm in my future with my perfect partner and I am so very grateful."** Let's be clear up front: I am not perfect, even my mama knew that. However, in my future my partner and I are together and we feel we really are perfect for each other. How wonderful! Love is surely blind, but it works perfectly for the two of us. How could this possibly happen? I have no idea how we got there, but in my future, she is there and I'm extremely grateful. So in my Movie I limit our interaction. She sits next to me on the couch and I pat her leg. I may visualize giving her an affectionate hip-bump at the kitchen counter. There may be more detail of us together in a vacation spot. Whatever the case, I don't look at her. I am not going to limit the possibilities. There are seven billion people on the planet and surely more than just one could be overwhelmingly perfect for me and me for her. I'm creating this in my future and it has to happen. Every day, I just give her a little pat and say how grateful I am. Sometimes I really feel the gratefulness and other times I feel nothing at all.

If you recall, when I started manifesting in my future, friends observed I was becoming much happier. There is the possibility that my perfect partner is me. No, I don't like myself that much. But I'm on my own and I've never been happier. I'm busy and fulfilled—so far so good. I'm certainly not giving up on the idea of meeting my perfect partner. I still give her an affectionate touch every day.

Either way, when I say I am grateful, I let the words flow like cream into coffee. I give my gratefulness time to make my thoughts even more powerful.

**"I'm in my future, on the computer looking at my bank account balances and the accounts are just FAT. I can't believe how much money is in there. I am so very grateful."** Once again I'm observing a future scene: I specify not having to worry about the month-to-month bill payments. I have multiple income streams and the equivalent of income that keeps my expenses paid way in advance. That feels really good! I have another scene where I have stacks of checks on the table. By the way, once I began visualizing those checks in my Movie, they began to appear in my life, stacked on that table in a couple of weeks. It doesn't happen every day but I'm very grateful. Hmmm... those checks could be coming electronically, too. I'm going to work on that.

**"I'm in my future and all of my time is perfectly synchronized. I am so very grateful."** I stay pretty busy. I like the activity but I used to take on too much. With my calendar filled, I found myself getting a little stressed out. I had a tiny amount of personal time and I wasn't doing all that I promised to do efficiently.

How could I fix something as complicated as that? Bingo! I didn't try to figure it out. Instead, I put the situation in my Movie and specified the perfect solution. I put out this instruction: "I'm in my future and all of my time is perfectly synchronized. I have all of the time needed for what I'm here to do, my career, my perfect partner, my friends and my own personal time. I never have to stress anymore to find hours in the day to do everything and still have time left over for myself." The change came about quickly. Within a couple weeks, I realized I was getting to bed earlier and playing solitaire on my iPad. (I had manifested all those cool electronics a year before.) What a difference! It really worked and it still works. After a little break I converted some of that solitaire time to writing time for this book. (By the way, did you notice where I slipped in the perfect partner?)

**"I'm in my future loving my perfect career. I am so very grateful."** Again I'm at the end of my day in the future observing my career. Notice I didn't say work, but chose the word career instead. In this way, I can see myself back home on the couch, resting and observing the elements of my perfect career. I can view my place of work as an office or at home. I visualize how happy and smoothly my vocations flow. I could be working on my own or with associates I respect and enjoy. I am appreciated, successful and financially rewarded.

**"I'm in my future, away from home and looking at the incredible scenery in this marvelous place. I don't have to worry about the time away or the money to be here. I am so very grateful."** Sometimes I visualize a room where I put my bags down, walk out to the balcony and hold that balcony rail. When I look out from the balcony I see just white. I won't limit where I am, so it could be anywhere that pleases me. Without seeing the view, I sometimes allow a non-visual impression of a beautiful sunset, mountains, stream, lake, ocean or all the above. I've allowed the possibility to experience locations I might not have chosen. You get to create the travel you wish. Don't hesitate to create your visual with high detail. Imagine where you want to go and put yourself in the scene. Add companions or your perfect partner if you like.

Within two to three months after I started envisioning my scene, I was surprised (so why am I still surprised?) to find myself holding a balcony rail looking at the Caribbean. I had been invited to attend a surprise birthday party for Judy at a private residence in the Dominican Republic. (I just have to add that Judy was not surprised. She's an intuitive and knew what we were up to, so the surprise was on us.) I only had to pay the airfare to be there and I enjoyed exceptional, private lodging with close friends for a week at no additional expense to me.

About eight weeks after that, I found myself in New York. I was given free airfare and a behind-the-scenes tour of the best Broadway play that year! So how did I get the free airfare? It starts with my perfect home, which is more than just a house: I specified that my house is not just for me but it is a gathering place for teachers, students and kind visitors. It is a sanctuary that is restful and peaceful. I'm the caretaker of the clubhouse so I get to sleep here and enjoy all the amenities.

Prior to this New York trip, a friend called and asked if I could host a visitor to the Denver area for a few days. I agreed because that's what my home is for. After spending time with this person, we quickly became friends. Before she left, she thanked me and said she wanted to do something for me. I declined and said there was no reason to do that. I was just happy we had met and became friends. "No, you don't understand," she said. "I work for an airline and I'm going to put you on my 'friends and family' list for free airline tickets. You can fly anywhere in the system for free as a standby passenger." I was incredulous, "What? Are you kidding me?" I told her about the vacation scene in my Movie and how I specified that money was not a problem to get there. We just laughed and laughed. I was in New York soon after, flying on that airline pass.

As I'm writing this, I'm sitting in Los Angeles where tonight I was invited to attend a movie premiere and party afterwards. My Movie scenes are manifesting themselves in fascinating ways and I look forward to future adventures. You had better believe that I still have my "travel scene" running.

### I've been constantly creating good things in my life.

Not everything has to be miraculous and dramatic: Things go smoothly, life is good. I'm happy and less encumbered by common problems. Add it all up and I feel the Movie has made a real difference in the direction of my life.

I want to be clear here. I'm taking responsibility for my present and my future. I'm being careful not to create negative situations or purposely mismanage the details of my life. I'm doing my part to allow my future to seamlessly appear.

You don't have to stick to your original script. Make changes and improvements as you go forward with your Movie. I have tweaked many scenes for the better and sometimes I see the changes take effect very quickly. It's all up to you, only you.

Manifesting in this way is a bit like stacking a sheet of copy paper on the "other side" every day. Some days the paper is perfect and others... well, the pages are a bit less than optimal. Each day you add another sheet of copy paper to the stack. Nicely done, you're doing great. One day a pretty ragged piece of paper goes on the pile, the next day is fine and then you forget a day. Every day another sheet of paper is added. On and on the stack grows. It's all forward progress and perfection is not required. It doesn't take long before a large amount of copy paper is stacked on the other side. This stack is much too substantial to exist in the non-physical state and it cascades over into the physical, into your precious life. Your thought has become real. It is as simple as that.

This is how your thoughts can bring about small or spectacular changes. Thought is just as real as rain or the hammer in your tool belt. Believe it or not, it is so.

## An Alternate Approach

Remember it's your Movie to make so it should be comfortable for you. I have a close friend who makes a big production of her Movie. Great idea! She goes into her movie theater, sits down and the show begins big time! The screen lights up with a fireworks-like display of shooting stars, rainbows and flowers. The show becomes more spectacular with words and sounds in many languages expressing gratefulness. What an opening! Once her scenes begin she seamlessly merges into the show on the screen, the lead actress in her fabulous production! She is the writer, producer, director and star of her own extravaganza.

## The Oops Factor

Invent what you like and be careful not to limit your intended result. There will be an outcome, so why create something that is less than your ideal? You have heard me mention the perfect this and the perfect that a number of times. Of course, use specifics whenever you like, but I much prefer the result that is beyond what I could have planned myself. I really respond to flawless when I see it!

One of the earliest results from my Movie is that I felt happier. I'm a pretty upbeat person, but my friends noticed that I was even happier than usual. When watching my Movie, I was happy of course, but this joy was spilling over into my life.

Perhaps it is easier and quicker to manifest joy rather than a new career. Perhaps there are fewer moving parts to arrange between those scenarios? Who knows? The Movie just works and I'm not the only one who sees the differences.

**Sometimes your Movie will bring you an unexpected outcome.**

It's very common for people to tell me that some of their friends have dropped away after they started working on a happier life in their future. The loss of the friendship was confusing and disappointing, but they weren't calling each other as often and perhaps there were communication problems. That happens, sometimes friends come and go, but when I asked them if they had made any new friends lately, they typically say yes. They say the friends that fell away were really not that close. Their bond wasn't as strong any longer and it was kind of a push for them to make time for each other. Sometimes these old friends or important relationships were really horrible. On the other hand, their new friends are more interesting, share more in common and are just more fun to be with. It is easy to make time for them.

Here is an extreme example of a very unexpected parting: For years I've been friends with two married women with children. The women know of each other but are not close. Neither of their marriages was very happy, but they all persevered. They had both been doing personal versions of the Movie for weeks when they received some startling news. They related this news to me in two separate phone calls, one day apart. They both told me their husbands wanted a divorce. It was a surprise they weren't ready for.

I was stunned as well. I waited a week to call them back. I was very concerned and I wanted to see how they were faring. In two separate, back-to-back phone calls they both said the same thing, "I haven't been this happy since high school."

They asked me what happened. I was pretty concerned about the possible problems I may have caused. I had been encouraging them to use thought to make their lives happier. "So, how long have you been doing the Movie? Have you been doing it every day?" I inquired.

Both women told me they did their Movie most every day for the last six weeks. I had to ask, "So in your Movie was your husband in any of those scenes?"

"Are you kidding?" they said. They went on to tell me that there was no way they would consider having that man in their happy visions. There was a stumble in their reply... "Oh my God, did I do that?" I couldn't know, but I offered that it was very possible. Further, this happened very quickly, in a matter of just a few weeks. Whatever the mechanism, the husbands apparently got it in their heads to leave for their own reasons. It was either a remarkable Movie outcome or one heck of a coincidence.

I offered, "Don't think for a moment that you are better than your husband. You leave him to his 'happy pond' and you enjoy yours. Support that thought as best as you can. Try to create a good ending so that you will have a new beginning for the two of you and the children."

What was the bottom line? Happiness was created, limits dropped away and the rest depends on what they dream up next!

My friends' divorces are just one possible outcome. Relationships can turn on a dime. There is the possibility that an uncomfortable relationship can mend and be made better. If you are struggling with a particular relationship, try putting together scenes of gladness with that person in your Movie. In your Movie, the dysfunctions of a couple or a family gathering can become the joyful opposite. In your

Movie, the difficulties with your significant other no longer exist. You two have so much in common and so many shared memories, why not have a Movie where you are both happy again? You don't have to specify if you are a couple or not in that future scenario. Just observe that you are both happy in the same room together. Don't limit the positive options.

So many touching stories result from manifesting the future.

I was talking to a good friend on a beautiful Colorado day. We were on my front deck listening to the waterfall below and everything seemed perfect, but there was a catch. My friend began telling me about unfortunate things in her life that seemed beyond her control. Her marriage was in serious trouble and so was her husband's business. Her father was doing his best, trying to help financially and with his business expertise. The business complications were creating distance between her and her father. She was carrying more burdens than can be spoken of here. She was working the problems as best as she knew how, asking, praying and hanging on. She was familiar with some manifesting approaches but hadn't tried them. I suggested the methods described here and her attitude was, "Why not? Things are pretty tough and out of my control. I'll give it a try."

During our hour-long conversation there were some laughs and tears. We put the idea of a Movie together and she was determined to chart a better future for herself and her son; a future that would include a very successful career on her own, her perfect partner and financial stability.

As we talked, a hummingbird flew right up to her face, moved around a bit and then flew off. Startled and amused, we began wrapping up our discussion. She was going to manifest a bright new future and give it her best shot. Suddenly, the hummingbird came right back, flew close to her face and looked her right in the eye. We were just amazed. The bird stared at her, moved a bit left to right, gave her one more straight-on good look and abruptly took off.

Whatever that was, it felt good. I was very hopeful for her future and my intentions were with hers.

# SIX

## Manifesting #2:
## Worry and Your Words

Great, you can create marvelous and thrilling results with the power of thought. You and those around you will see things unfold and share spectacular stories! Yes you will. Ah, but there is a catch. Isn't there always a catch? Yes, but...

Your thoughts create and they are creating all the time. You put a lot of chaff into the air, thousands of random and repetitive thoughts every day. It's okay. Generally, it is the things you focus on repetitively that manifest. Those countless other words and images are not going to create anything unless you keep them in your consciousness over and over. If you are constantly allowing someone to get under your skin, then it becomes part of your field. You will create a Movie of that unease as you go forward. Get the repetitive junk out of your current environment or at least don't let it get to you. Eliminate or downgrade it as best you can. Be responsible and then be magical. Make sure that when you imagine your future these problems don't exist there.

By repeating the preferred thoughts you want in your Movie each day, those intentions will begin to form up in your life. Sweet! But there's another theme that runs through all of those thousands of thoughts we have each day...

## We Worry

Worries are thoughts as well. We can create anything with worry, and guess what? Worries are thoughts that are emotionally loaded with FEAR. We are constantly thinking randomly and repetitively. Some of those thoughts are the worries that continue to come to mind again and again throughout the day. Since we keep touching these thoughts and load them emotionally, they will begin to manifest physically.

**Remember those two great forces: love and fear.**

I wonder how much unease we create with worry and fear? How much negativity would you like to invite into your life? Whatever force that makes thought manifest, it creates without judgment. You are free to make all the things you wish, good and bad, large and small. Keep your mind clear of the negatives. You can create a negative result by repetitively thinking about those worrisome concerns and problems.

If only we could just stop worrying. Forget about it, right? Get over it. Don't think about it, please!

It is a rare person who can successfully handle those big fat worries. Methods abound to diminish worry and they can be really effective. We can take on big problems through our own force of will, diminish their importance or embrace prayer and faith. I have tried many methods with varying degrees of success, but some problems can really get to me and bring on the worrying anyway.

Envision yourself worrying about something in the middle of the night. It's a bothersome piece of information, a big deal. What are your options at 3 a.m.? Are you going to wake someone at that hour to talk it over and help you solve the problem? Will you lay awake and stare at the ceiling in full worry mode? Get up and pace the floor? Pray? Cry?

Worry is a thought and your thought is emotionally loaded with fear. If you have a big worry then you have a big intention. Your thoughts can create negative or positive results, so let's work on not allowing your negative worries to create undesirable outcomes.

Return to the scenario where you are driving your car to the museum. Your hands are on the wheel and you're happily moving to your destination with the confidence that you're going to get there. It is highly likely you're going to arrive just fine.

Now let's observe you steering the car in full worry mode. Instead of confidently going forward, your car is now in reverse at 70 miles an hour on the interstate! Your worries are creating the *opposite* of what you want and they are taking you into the traffic where unknown consequences abound.

You can't afford to have these negative things develop in your life. How can you stop this backward slide?

The quick answer is to stop worrying about them. By whatever method, diminish them in your mind so that you don't have this negative, recurring thought. Again, there are some strategies for this but I haven't found them to be very effective in the long run. Most of us like things just so, all the little ducks lined up in a row. If one of those little ducklings gets out of line, we will fuss and worry until that little guy is back in line. We are so trained to worry. However, there is something we can do to convert our tendency to worry into a wonderful asset.

## Convert Your Worries to Action Items

Think of something that's worrying you.

**Now, put it on your to-do list or calendar.**

If you have a pain in your right shoulder, quit worrying about it day after day. Put it on your calendar. Quit carrying that worry, take action and quickly decrease the odds of some really bad medical news coming your way. I feel like a doctor myself when I say, "There now, doesn't that feel better?" You can diminish the worry now. Put it on the calendar to call your doctor and make an appointment. When the reminder comes up, call the office. If you're unavailable to phone in then, move your reminder forward, but keep it on your calendar as an action item until you make a confirmed appointment with the doctor. In the meantime leave it alone, that's the point. Don't load it up emotionally with your worry or imagine unpleasant scenarios. There's nothing else to do until you sit down with the doctor at your appointed time. You have taken action and made the appointment. You have converted your worry to nothing more than a date on your calendar.

Money problems? What can you possibly do about it at 3 a.m.? Well for one thing, you have to stop that worry quickly. By repeating that anxious thought, you can make that lack of money a reality. Instead, you should think in terms of action. Perhaps someone owes you money. Make a mental or written note to call that person in the morning. Decide to take action by asking your boss for that raise. Maybe it's time to launch your scheme for earning extra income. These are all positive options. Convert that worry to a line item on your to-do list or place it in your calendar. Quit carrying an emotionally loaded thought that can take you where you don't want to go.

You made a positive move. Your worries are now to-do items, just neutral dates on your calendar. This is a fabulous way to get the worries off your shoulders. You haven't neglected any responsibility, you're not dealing with everything all at once and you're not fueling these concerns with negative emotions.

It took me a few weeks to get in the mode of not worrying. First, I used the trick of using the word "concern" rather than "worry" and that did help some.

After a few weeks, I got better at alleviating worry. If a concern popped up, I immediately took action or scheduled the item into the calendar. It felt good. I could pat myself on the back for taking action and making forward progress. "Good doggie!"

If you have a powerful worry neutralizer that works for you, then use it. However you can, don't worry negative thoughts into existence and remember...

**You can go to the future to take care of those concerns!**

Need new tires? Write it on your calendar: Put new tires on the car. If you can't afford to put tires on the car Wednesday, just continue to move the item forward on your calendar. Then go to the future every day and notice your tires are not an issue, ever. Stay with it until the appointed day comes for you to get your new tires.

Your job is not going well? In your Movie you are very successful with your career, well-respected, financially rewarded and admired.

I really like this one: A call comes in. It's really not good news. Hang up, look at that phone and say, "This problem is going into my Movie tomorrow and it won't exist!"

Problems come in a lot of forms: health, relationships, money, safety, careers, time management, etc. This is life on earth and problems come in an endless stream. Put the issues and worries you face into your list or calendar for action. Next, create a scenario in your Movie without those concerns or view them completed. What a grateful moment!

You are no longer the one driving backwards on the highway. You are dealing with these concerns in a responsible, organized and positive way. You may not like these troubles, but you manage them as needed and organize the rest in a way that doesn't overwhelm you. Congratulations! You are only creating the things you choose.

Fear may not have been conquered, that's a lot to ask, but you will observe that it is considerably diminished in your life. Here is another powerful tool at your disposal:

## Your Words

It is very important to match your words to your vision. Create an advantage by synchronizing the future you are creating with your present actions. In the present, your actions and words are as powerful as thoughts. Take every advantage and synchronize your present to your terrific future.

**Make an effort to choose your words carefully.**

When you say, "I'm thinking about it" or "I'm going to" you have manifested nothing new, only the command to stay in place. You are gonna, maybe, um, later. Instead of, "I'm thinking about getting a new car," say something much more powerful: "I see myself driving that perfect car." Rather than, "I want to get a really good job," match what you are seeing in your Movie and say, "I'm moving toward my perfect career!" Avoid "I really need that air-conditioner fixed." With that statement you have commanded yourself to be needy. Ouch! Try instead, "I am having that air-conditioner fixed," or "I will have that air conditioner fixed."

Don't be wanting or needy. Those statements are weak forces. See yourself receiving instead and forcefully moving toward the future of your creation. When you are wanting or needing, then you are loading yourself for failure. If your words are about wanting or needing something then you have made the command to remain in a place of want or need.

Managing your words is an acquired skill. Don't think badly of yourself when you trip on a word. Be aware that your thoughts and words have power, but give yourself some slack, please! Break the cycle of repeating negative and weak words. Choose more positive statements in your day and keep manifesting the future you want.

# SEVEN

## And You Don't Need #3: Who You Really Are

I still remember the day I was explaining this way of manifesting to a friend. I was in my study on the phone, sitting comfortably and looking at a wall of bookshelves. I was wrapping up the explanation about dealing with fear when a new thought began streaming into my head. It was clearly a new idea, fully formed and insisting to be expressed. I just gave in and allowed this idea to flow into the conversation.

"You know, all of those woo-woo, guru books, all of those self-help and metaphysical seminars, all of the Sunday school instruction and late-night discussions over wine about how things work? They generally come down to a few simple truths. One of those concepts, and to many it is a true thing, is that if we could be who we fully are, our higher selves, we could do anything. We could walk on water, we could move mountains, we could turn water into wine."

I subscribe to that, but it is near-impossible to achieve that state of being, your higher self. It would certainly be difficult to be all that you are for the length of your entire Movie.

Pretend that you are going to your personal Movie theater and I'm standing at the front door, making sure that you have everything in order. I'm there to ensure that you are at full strength, your highest possible self. You aspire to be all that you are. Nothing is left to chance, so that when you go into to your theater and run your Movie everything you imagine will happen. Your higher self can make miracles happen instantly and that is why you are there.

At the theater door, I carefully look you over. "That's good," I say, "You have been taking care of yourself. I see you've been on a stringent diet. Excellent, and you're wearing all white. Nicely done. Good, good. So, have any impure thoughts?" Oh that damn buzzer went off! Too bad, your impure thoughts disqualify you from going in. You are not at full potential.

Don't worry; you don't have to be perfect to see your perfect Movie. There is an easier way.

**I observe that when I'm in my Movie I've never been so powerful.**

Instead of facing the bouncer, I am like a 3-year-old that skips the front door, goes around the theater and enters though the side door. Once I'm in the theater, I can run my Movie every time. I'm a small child watching my Movie. I don't intellectualize or doubt the possibility of what I'm seeing. I just watch the show. It flows all over me and I'm happy to be there. Nothing gets in the way and I don't judge what I'm seeing. I just watch the Movie.

You see yourself in your future and it's just fabulous. In scene after scene, you are in your future without judgment or trying to calculate how you got there. You just accept what you're seeing and experience what it feels like. It's an emotional experience at times and you feel very happy. You are actually creating your future by walking around in your scenes and powering them emotionally with gratitude.

## Your Power

We are more powerful than we understand. Regular folks have seen their higher selves or experienced who they truly are at full strength. Witnesses have often reported seeing their friends or acquaintances in supernatural ways. Stories of this kind are not that rare. These visual and emotional experiences are witnessed in dreams, visions and in wide-awake experiences. Sometimes people observe their friends as very tall and dressed in a robe or the friend may seem to be floating and translucent. Others describe a person they recognize, solid-physical in their home but the person they saw was thousands of miles away at the time.

I have seen this phenomenon for myself and so have some of my acquaintances. Truly, if you could see who you really are in full form, you would be stunned at the power, potential and the love that you hold and project. We are all capable of amazing feats.

If your higher self walked into a restaurant, all of us inside would hit the ground without thinking: We would know you were God or someone Very Big. We could not imagine anything more powerful than you and we would react in reverence. That is the potential in you, in me, in the baby going by in the stroller. We are so much bigger than we understand or can comprehend.

This life on earth is very convincing, but beyond our physical selves we are free, spiritual beings without limits. At times we are like fish out of water, flopping on the beach and gasping for air. It would be comical if our lives weren't so painful and confusing at times. If we could see the larger picture, we would only be moderately concerned with our troubles, knowing that we can get out of any jam and resolve any problem. We are fully empowered to manipulate the world around us with our thoughts, words and actions.

### So, you don't need #3.

The potential of our higher selves is an interesting theory, but it's not necessary to your success. Don't go into your Movie thinking you have to be a perfect Supergirl or Superman. You're just going to trip up on your own cape. All you have to do is quietly flow through the parts of your Movie as a child would do, and nothing exceptional of you is required.

**You now have your direction. You know what you want to create for yourself.**

You have your hands on the wheel, so be smart.

**Point yourself to happiness.**

# EIGHT

## Get Ready:
## It Is Already Happening

At times you may observe your Movie starting to flow over into the physical world in a small way. It's not the full-blown event you're waiting for but a snippet, a clue that the future you're working on may be just around the corner. An analogy would be that you dropped something onto your outer garment and it bled into the next one, flowing across the boundary.

For example, I have heard the story a number of times about men and women putting that perfect partner into their Movie. Their search for a significant other had been in a drought condition for some time. Later I hear that they have bumped into some interesting people via friends, at parties or by sheer coincidence. Suddenly, they are steadily meeting attractive people. Some have said they're too busy to date people who aren't perfect for them. Others observed they really liked someone at first, but after some time they definitely knew this person was not The One. A few people catch on to what is being manifested, and others fall into a sort of complaint. It always makes me chuckle and I offer, "Isn't this what you were going for? You worked to meet that perfect partner and now interesting people are starting to roll in." One could make the case that the "perfect partner" intention is starting to manifest, to flow over into the physical world.

If I chat with these folks a bit more, they admit they are learning something from the process. They find a new person is really not compatible with them after the first few meetings. But with each new person they learn more about themselves and what's really important in their lives. I've been there and I'm doing that! Surprisingly, a number of traits that seemed unattractive before are now more acceptable with these new companions and other characteristics are absolutely, positively NOT!

Sometimes, love appears then disappears. For whatever reasons, a relationship doesn't hold. Some are saddened by the experience and others feel rejuvenated. Regardless, something important has happened to those lucky people. Their hearts opened. They felt love. Everything works just as it should. Lightning struck, the impossible found them and it's entirely probable that love will find them again.

A new acquaintance told me an interesting experience recently. This man had not been in a loving relationship for a very long time. He wondered if it was his fault; that somehow he was getting in the way of having the serious relationship he desired. He felt like his heart was encased in steel and unable to care, he said. Then came an event that turned his thinking around. He met the 2½-year-old daughter of his neighbor and was instantly smitten. The little girl took to him also and now they enjoy a wonderful friendship.

Since she is not family, they don't get to see each other frequently, but the girl definitely opened his heart and demonstrated the possibilities of love finding him again. With a renewed hope, he is working to manifest his perfect partner.

When friends mention they are starting to encounter more interesting people or falling in love for a time, I like to say they are on the right bus. They are working an intention for their perfect partner so it follows that more meaningful people are coming into their lives—getting on the bus. New and interesting friends are made. Amazing! Those that are paying attention remark that the drought is apparently over and they relax.

Something new is flowing and moving in their favor. Some of these new acquaintances set the bar a bit higher. This person is not quite that perfect One but he or she is like a template for what the ideal companion would be. It gets better: The person they are seeking is also seeking them. Their perfect partner may be at the next stop.

Here's a recent example. About a year ago, I met a delightful woman at a gallery exhibition of my art works. She had previously worked at this gallery but we had never met. She went out of her way to be there and I was delighted that she liked my exhibit. Part of my responsibility that night was to spend a little time with everyone in conversation and thank them for coming to my show. It was a busy night, so the woman and I didn't have a lot of time for conversation. After the exhibit, I asked her if she wanted to go to the restaurant next door so we could talk more.

We had a lovely conversation over a number of topics. The conversation came around to asking or wishing for better in our lives. She was someone who did put forward requests or prayers. One of her wishes was to find her good companion and partner, so I began to talk about manifesting. I recommended that she put forward the idea of her perfect partner.

Recently, I attended an important event, her wedding reception. I met her husband, a wonderful man, and it is a delight to see the two of them so happy together. I stole a moment to ask her, "So after we met did you continue to do the manifesting idea we spoke of?"

"Yes," she said.

Another question, "So did you use the term 'perfect partner' when you were manifesting?"

She gazed up a bit, then smiled and said, "Yes I did."

Pretty good so far, I thought, "And did you do your manifesting every day and include your perfect partner?"

"I did. Right up until the day we got married." She smiled and glowed as only brides can do.

Her new husband told me that she just came to his mind one day and he felt the urge to try to find her using the social networks. They had attended high school together and he successively located her on the one network where she used her maiden name. She listed some professional expertise with computers so he contacted her requesting help with his. I laughed out loud and we gave each other a congratulatory high five. Turns out there wasn't a computer problem at all, but two very good people did find their perfect partners.

## Increase the Chances

You are doing your Movie every day, excellent! Now you should go downstairs, turn off the phones and lock the door, right? Of course not. Live your normal life but be observant. Your thoughts are changing things around you. You may be invited to more events and meet new people. These are all opportunities for you to be in a better position to receive what you are manifesting.

You may be presented with a new job opportunity, important health information, who knows? Be assured that what you seek is moving your way. Change your limiting patterns. Not everything in your Movie can find you by calling you or walking through your front door. Work smart, get out and increase the odds for a good result. Be in the world and let your wonderful future find you. Do not put yourself in highly uncomfortable or dangerous situations, that is not in your Movie, and it's completely unnecessary.

When you continue your Movie, you'll begin to see improvements in your life. If you were to graph your progress, you wouldn't see a perfectly upward 45-degree angle. Life has its ups and downs even if you are a smashing success. This isn't heaven on earth, so there will be the usual peaks and valleys. However, your life will be different because you will be creating something more positive. Once you begin your Movie, your graph with the peaks and valleys will remain, but the overall trend-line of your graph is upward.

You're not doing this alone. Yes, you are creating these future scenarios, but notice that others are helping. You may be meeting new people, encountering important ideas and receiving helpful coincidences. Because you say yes more, you will find yourself in different places with new faces, experiences, the opportunities required for your new life. You are making miracles and moving mountains, right?

**Do you know how to move mountains? Get a lot of ants.**

## Planting the Flag

Intentions are powerful. If you are doing your Movie, making lists or vision boards, you are adding layers of intention to your thought and your thought is building from that wisp of vapor into something more solid. Don't forget, gratitude is a big magnifier of intentions, so always add gratefulness in your Movie and in your life.

After the first edition of this book was published, stories came in from readers, and an interesting trend emerged. Let's call it Planting the Flag. It is another way to increase your intention by going one step further.

In the story that follows, Nancy decides to use the *Manifesting 1, 2, 3* techniques and something more. To reach her goal of being better known as an artist and selling her works, she was prepared to put some skin in the game. In this case, she describes manifesting her successful future each day and paying to advertise her work. That's good, basic business with manifesting mixed in.

For the next part of her plan, she visualized and manifested an article in the same magazine, a real coup. She included that article in her Movie every day and to make it happen, she was prepared to buy even more expensive advertising. She was specifying an event in her future and increasing the power of her intention with the commitment of writing a check, should that event take place.

What we think or imagine is powerful and gratefulness makes it more so. What we say and do in the physical world has great influence as well. Our positive words and actions will aid the creation of positive outcomes, with negativity doing the opposite. Which is stronger, thinking something nice about someone or saying it out loud to that person? Your spoken words will produce an immediate effect with the person you are talking to and the words will have an effect on you as well.

When you are Planting a Flag, your mind and physical actions are combined. You're manifesting a future event and at the same time, you're willing to commit to a physical action. It might be putting more time into a project or writing that check. It may feel like a stretch to do so, but when the event happens, you will follow through with the physical action. These two strong intentions, one of the mind and another linking to the physical world, point you to where you want to go: It's where the flag is.

## Nancy Explains

After 20 years of working in the corporate world, I quit my job to pursue a career in art full-time. It was many years in coming: I'd been a part-time painter since I was 17 and was finally in a place to give art my full attention.

One of the first things I decided to do to promote my work was take out a series of three, 1/2 page ads in a major western art publication. This was not inexpensive, but I felt it important to put my name and work "out there" as much as possible. The first ad came out in the summer. I sold one painting as a result of that first ad. That was OK, but not quite what I'd hoped.

At this point, I decided to use one of Ken Elliott's techniques called "Planting a Flag." My flag would be, "If this western art magazine writes an article about me, I will buy a full-page ad from them." Honestly, I figured that my chances of this particular art magazine doing an article on me and my work was pretty slim after just a few months of painting full-time, but I thought, "What the heck, I have absolutely nothing to lose in trying." I added that flag to my daily Movie immediately.

Six weeks later, I phoned the magazine ad representative to ask about advertising rates for the coming year. I told her about the sales I'd had as a result of the recent ad in the magazine. By this time I had sold an additional four paintings from my advertising campaign and toyed with the idea of more ads for next year. I ended the conversation with the new pricing in hand, but I had not committed to any more ads by that point. I needed time to think about it. This was a lot of money. Each 1/2 page ad cost about $2,400.

About a week later, the ad rep called me back and said that she had exciting news: The magazine's editor really liked my work and wanted to do an article on me and my art in the March issue.

I think my jaw hit the floor. I was actually speechless! Seven weeks after I planted a flag, and only a few months as a full-time artist, this very well-known western art publication wanted to do an article on me. Wow.

Needless to say, I said YES to the article and also signed up for a one-page ad before we ended the conversation.

A few days later, the ad rep emailed me and sweetened the deal a bit. She and the editor wanted to give me a free 1/2 page ad in this year's Christmas issue. Yes, free. No strings attached, just free.

OK, sign me up!

I have come away from this realizing just how powerful planting even a small flag can be, so I am planting even bigger flags now. I can't wait to see what happens. I am very grateful to Spirit and everyone involved!

# NINE

## The Bonus:
## Grateful Things

I've heard it said in many ways:

**Happiness is a side effect of gratefulness.**

You don't have to be a Pollyanna to bring a little more happiness into your life. The simple act of being appreciative can make your attitude and your day a little better. Being grateful leads to positive acts like chatting up the store clerk or remembering to say a simple "thank you" more often. Everybody gets this concept, it's nothing new. We have already discussed that gratefulness is an important component in your Movie. But there is more. The act of being grateful can be further focused and used to your benefit.

I have always been a little above average in the grateful category. Before I heard about this bonus, I was very satisfied and really had no thoughts or compelling reasons to raise my level of gratitude. But then I came across something Judy Goodman said in a lecture. To my mind, it was a throwaway line, something I had heard in many times in different ways. It was a sweet little bit of Philosophy 101 and not of much value to me at the time. She said,

**"Every day, think of seven Grateful Things."**

I didn't recognize that pearl of wisdom. I didn't feel the urge to use the information, nor did I value the advice as something important, so I just forgot about it. Then came the day that I was gazing out the window of my perfect home.

## My Junkyard

I was very happy and very fortunate to be in my ideal house. I had many to thank, did so and then my mind went blank. The thought came to me that my life was perfect right out to the curb line. Everything was just as it should be and I was very happy and comfortable inside that perimeter. My world inside was peaceful and a dream come true. This was the world I was presently aware of.

Beyond my curb was an unpredictable world with trillions of moving parts. Then it hit me. Maybe I was having a psychic episode, but I clearly understood that just outside the curb line was my own personal junkyard. Beyond my present awareness was another zone of things I no longer considered but they were a part of me just the same. In this case I was given a gentle representation of the negative things I was carrying around. There was a LOT of junk!

I couldn't really see, but what I perceived was the equivalent of an unsavory pile of old metal parts, tangled up barbed wire and scattered litter everywhere. I clearly had the sense of my small-time personal garbage. Beyond my usual awareness was a landscape cluttered with all I hadn't dealt with or forgiven. It was the litter from my past and as minor as it was, I was unconsciously shouldering this load and creating limits for myself.

My old personal rubbish was everywhere, just out of sight until now. It was embarrassing. Some of this trash might have represented negative interactions I had with someone. I was getting the impression that I couldn't see it, but other people were remembering those events. Ouch!

It was now a couple of months after Judy's lecture and curiously, her advice came back to me at that moment: "Every day, think of seven Grateful Things."

Prompting wasn't required, I went right to it. I stood there and quickly came up with seven items I'm very pleased to have in my life.

I'm grateful for:
My perfect health
My perfect home
The marvelous people and teachers throughout my life
My successful career as an artist
My ability to travel

I'm grateful that:
I'm doing what I'm here to do
I'm not concerned about my finances

I let those Grateful Things flow from my heart and I went back to my day.

The next afternoon, I looked over to the same window and remembered the junk-fest of the day before. I stood in the same spot, looked out the window and cleared my mind.

By some feeling or intuition, I had a real impression that everything beyond the curb line was clear. This sense was very different from just looking out the window and not having any sensation at all. I was clearly getting a gut feeling that my junkyard had vanished. I was elated. I realized that I had been limiting myself. These bits of negativity had been holding me back and I may have been underperforming in some way.

I felt like all around me was a Teflon-coated runway for my incoming intentions. There were no obstructions around me in any direction and it felt terrific. Woo hoo!

## The Extra Mile

Acknowledging my seven Grateful Things was like going the extra mile. It was a bonus and it made a difference. At a minimum, it made me happier. You can't avoid feeling better when you acknowledge the good that surrounds you.

I can't precisely gauge if my intentions came in better and quicker as a result of the Grateful Things. I feel like they did, but it could be the cumulative effects of the weeks in my Movie.

Regardless, repeating seven Grateful Things every day will give you perspective. You will become happier from taking the time to appreciate the goodness presently in your life. It only takes a small bit of time every day to be more joyfully aware and alive.

As you take note of your Grateful Things, don't leave out happy occurrences and successes from your past either. You can be grateful for the award you were given, the big sale last year, or that big boost of confidence from a childhood moment. Your gratefulness for past events clears the way and makes it easier for them to happen again.

Further, the Grateful Things contain many of the same thoughts as your Movie. As you gratefully revisit some of the same Movie items, you layer on more intention and create more powerfully. Your Grateful Things are felt emotionally, reinforcing and assisting your Movie. You are gratefully reasserting the positives in your life: It's a win-win situation!

Minding your seven Grateful Things each day is easy to do. You can go through your seven Grateful Things at almost any time or place. Eyes open or shut, it can be anywhere you have a space for clear thought: walking around the house or sitting in a waiting room. It's easy to be grateful anywhere. Your grateful thoughts can quickly be inserted all at once or bit by bit into your day. Do your Grateful Things before your Movie and you have covered all the bases at the same time. Some find that they like splitting the two activities, going into grateful modes more than once a day.

Also, don't make the number seven an absolute rule. Remember this is all about intention, so any grateful thing you do is a positive. Some days I may not get to seven things and on others I may do many more. Don't be concerned about hitting the number on the nose.

Use the seven Grateful Things to increase your happiness and help make the way clear for the intentions of your future.

# TEN

## Before You Take Off: Useful Bits

Lucky you! Now you are empowered to do amazing things for yourself. You don't have to wait for anything else but just in case, here are some helpful tips.

Back to Daffy Duck. I treated what I had learned like a trick. I never thought about using the power of thought for myself. I was very slow on the uptake, but I finally realized if I continued to send Judy that duck every day she would get it in a physical form. How? Perhaps some little girl would see Judy in the produce section of the grocery store, walk up to her and put a Daffy Duck sticker right on her leg. Or a courier will ring her doorbell and present her with a box containing a stuffed Daffy Duck! If you stay with your intention, it will happen. It is the law and it will happen every time.

### Before you start your Movie, know what you require.

What are your priorities? Don't be concerned with how something you desire could possibly happen. In your future you are already enjoying that relationship, place or thing. Imagine all the positive outcomes and be in it. You are deserving, worthy and empowered to bring happiness and comfort into your life.

### Do your Movie and seven Grateful Things every day.

Make these daily practices a priority. It is one of the most important things we can do. You will see and feel the results of these actions. Your thoughts will bring things to you more quickly and sometimes in ways you would never plan. This is the shortcut, the way to bring what you require to you on the diagonal. You are in your future and you are so grateful.

### Be grateful to God or the God of your understanding.

We have all thought about creation from time to time. How did all of this happen? Is it an exquisite accident, a result of chance? Did all there is come from a great mind? Regardless of your opinion or belief, why not thank the creator that made it possible? It's just good manners and it leaves a nice feeling. If all of this was pure chance, then give a smile and wink in response to the well-ordered world you live in. Either way, lucky us!

### Don't judge yourself.

I have a sneaking feeling that many people do their Movie better than I do. Could I do this more efficiently? You bet, but it doesn't matter. I get it done, I'm on it every day, and I get spectacular results anyway. I fall asleep, wander, miss a day, and in some scenes, forget to be grateful. I'm a visual artist, so I get involved in the look of my future scenes and forget the grateful part. I often have to revisit my scenes to say, "Oh yes, and I'm very grateful for this, this and this." I am good to myself. I don't judge myself harshly. Since I am steadily doing my Movie and seven Grateful Things, progress is being made. I will reach my destination every time. A high score is not required for success, only repetitive and positive action.

### What's the best method for envisioning a Movie?

To prepare for my Movie, I choose a time when I'm sitting up. The chances are far greater that I'm alert and awake. I find when I'm doing the Movie laying down I will often go to sleep because we are trained to do that. I prefer to recline, but only do so if I'm not tired. Either way, I'm just as normal as anyone else. My mind wanders and pink elephants appear in my thoughts. I'm not at all concerned if my thinking veers off to another subject during my Movie. I don't sit down every day and repeat a vision of pink elephants. Without the repetition and intention, I won't have any elephants in my future.

### How should I feel?

On a few occasions I have felt so grateful in response to my Movie that I've been brought to tears. Emotions are a very powerful manifestation tool so allow yourself to feel. Most of the time your emotions will be a combination of feeling a little something or nothing at all. That is perfectly normal. At the end of your scene when you say, "I am so grateful," give the words a little time to work their magic. Here is that phrase again, "Let the gratefulness flow like cream into coffee."

When you are in your future, every sense you bring into play creates more powerfully. When you are in your future scene, touch some of the objects around you. Smell the flowers, touch the tabletop, notice the sounds of traffic near your sidewalk café. All of your senses are important elements to more powerfully create your future.

**Your good intentions may not come exactly when you prefer or in exactly the form you specify.**

Here's a common phrase: fear of failure. Do yourself a favor and don't quit before you even start. Without any experience or prior knowledge, my attempts at manifesting got results. Has everything I've imagined come to pass yet? No, but I am in the game, on the field and working it every day. Manifesting is not a pass/fail course. Your creations are all works in progress, evolving in different ways and at various times.

We have all failed hundreds of times in our lives but we have muddled through somehow. Many of the greatest lessons in life come through failure and pain. When events don't go the way we plan or want, we learn something valuable. Don't be afraid to create the future you want. I'm not trying to caution you that bad things will happen. I'm submitting that you may arrive via an unexpected but valuable route.

Many of us intend to find that perfect partner or companion. We set the bar high or we certainly should. Does everyone find that ideal person immediately? Of course not. Our perfect partner is likely a match for who we are now and not the person we were years ago. Since we are going for perfect, we may require just a bit more polishing before the perfect partner appears. Watch for an uptick in the quality of the people you meet. With each new person you will likely learn a little more about your potential partner and yourself. Perhaps this is all part of the polishing process, becoming more "perfect" for that perfect companion. The appearance of these fascinating people indicates you may be heading in the right direction, so keep the bar high, don't settle for Mr. or Ms. Less-Than, be patient and enjoy the ride.

Let's say you are 14 years old and you are expecting a red Maserati. It is highly likely there may be a wait involved for the real thing, but keep an eye out for a Maserati poster or the model replica dropping into your life.

Perhaps you are suffering from any number of maladies or find yourself in a tough situation. By all means, use all of the suggestions in this book to gain the advantage or your cure. Everyone has their afflictions, everyone has their issues. Have you noticed that we all have experienced pain? No one gets a free pass but each of these experiences provides us with an opportunity to become who we aspire to be. Whenever we are presented with hardship or challenges, we get to decide at that moment how to react. We are creating who we are and how we are perceived minute to minute, every day.

You may not have the perfect cure available to you. It may turn out that your difficult situation will take years to play out. It is up to you to decide how to accept and respond to the difficulty. Regardless, go into your Movie every day and walk around in your perfect future, free of the burden. There will be a result because your thoughts are real. A number of things can happen. You may realize that this pain or burden has been diminished to a point where you're not overwhelmed. You might feel lighter and less burdened. Perhaps the realization emerges that this is not a punishment. Some have an epiphany. It's as if they see with a greater view and realize that their malady is a permanent feature, but less important in their lives. They come to the realization that all this hardship is not wasted. Perhaps they have become the teacher of that affliction.

We can discover more happiness and joy regardless of our circumstances. This is a miracle in its own way. Sometimes the wisdom and peace in one's heart is far more precious than the cure and that may be the perfect end result.

### Can I manifest for other people?

Perhaps. Can you take the algebra test for your son? Here's the deeper question, should you? You can certainly manifest things for yourself and when you do so it affects the field around you. If you become happier, it might affect the happiness of others. If you move into the perfect apartment or your wonderful new career, then it affects the life of your landlord and colleagues to some degree.

Why not put the people you're concerned about in your movie and see them in your future as happy and fulfilled? Don't even try to formulate how they came into their happiness. Just be joyful with them in your future. If I intend to manifest or pray for other people, I will always go for the cure or the best result, but I really don't know what's best for someone else. How could I possibly know what is the best path in their lives? To quote Judy Goodman, "Ask for their best and highest outcome."

### What is best? Wish lists, vision boards or the Movie?

A case has been made for all three, but my bias is towards the Movie. The Movie is much closer to a physical reality and uses all the senses and emotions you want to put into it. Lists and vision boards are much less so. But let's not limit any possibility. You can use your senses to power up a list or vision board item. We are really talking about layers of intention here so why not use all three? Add sensory information and emotions where you can. With the tools in this book you will increase your odds for success. You have a distinct advantage now, so use it.

### What can be manifested?

Look at the skyline of a great city. A thought preceded the laying of every street and every skyscraper. Unless it occurred naturally and was preserved as a natural space, it was first conceived and planned by us. The entire upward skyline was first a thought that looked like a wisp of vapor, nothing more. As more intentions and people joined that intention, infrastructure and buildings rose out of the ground.

Everything in the room around you was an idea that started as a wisp in the unseen field around you. You have been creating things with thought all your life and it is allowed that you can create anything.

### What should I ask for? Be smart!

That is totally up to you, thank goodness! You are free to create anything without limits. Create an excess in your life of joy and affluence and give the extra away. Overflow your cup and share if you like. Go beyond the minimum and fly. I find myself asking for a number of good things throughout the day and at times I may feel anxious with some requests. There is that phrase, "Be careful what you ask for."

Here is a cautionary story from a few months ago: Two friends and I went out for dinner one night. We were enjoying ourselves in conversation and included our waitress from time to time. Our talk turned to manifesting, and when our waitress overheard a bit of what we were saying, she nodded in approval. "So do you ask or wish for things to come into your life?" I asked her.

"Funny you should ask that," she said with a faraway look on her face. "A month ago I was asking to be in a car wreck."

"What?" we all asked in unison, shocked.

The waitress said a few months earlier her girlfriend had been in-before you take off

volved in a car accident. Apparently the girlfriend came away with little or no injuries and with another bit of good fortune. She received a monetary settlement as a result of the collision. Our waitress didn't disclose the amount but apparently the payment provoked an idea.

"So, you were wishing for a car wreck so you could get a cash settlement?" I asked.

She had a half smile and ironic look on her face. It was obvious she had given this a lot of thought. "Yes, it's seemed like a pretty good idea at the time," she said.

The three of us were in a state of disbelief. We were in the manifesting choir. All of us had talked about intention and positive thoughts many times. We would never in our wildest dreams put out an intention like that.

Our minds registered an alarm but we started laughing at the absurdity of her request. Like waiting for a man to step on a banana peel, we wanted to know what was coming next, but part of us did not want to know. We leaned forward..."So?"

"Two weeks ago I was crossing the street and I got hit by a car."

"You're kidding!" I said. "You weren't in a car. You were a pedestrian and got hit by a car?"

I'm glad she kept that grin. "Yes, I was walking across the street and got hit. I'm okay though. It was very minor and everything turned out alright."

"I can't believe you did that," I said as we all laughed with relief. "Obviously you needed the money. Did you get a settlement?"

"No," she said, "but I did learn a good lesson."

### *What should I ask for? Be positive!*

I love good stories, so here is one more that is a terrific example of making change and creating miracles.

A few years ago, a younger couple I know called me. They had heard me discuss manifesting techniques previously, and were now in a jam over their mortgage. Could they come over and discuss manifesting again? A couple days later, we met at my house.

They have two wonderful children and their lives are centered in service to others. Each of them owns a single-employee business. Times were bad economically and their businesses had suffered mightily. They found themselves struggling to pay their mortgage held by one of the largest banks in the country. The three of us sat together and I offered all of the manifesting information you have read here. The couple returned home, inspired to do their Movie every day.

Three or four months later, a mutual friend indicated she had talked with this couple about financial matters and they mentioned my name. The mutual friend did not want to discuss these private affairs and recommended that I contact the couple right away. I was concerned about talking to them. What if I had given advice or information that was detrimental to them? I called and the husband told the most amazing story. The couple had been doing their Movie every day for weeks. In their Movies, each of them created a future in their perfect house without financial problems.

Still, business had continued to get worse and they found themselves two months behind in their mortgage payments. They called their bank to admit the obvious: Money was owed and their financial future was bleak. Since each of their income streams was way down, the couple would be ineligible to refinance. They were at the mercy of the bank and asked what could possibly be done to keep their house. The bank representative agreed to call the couple back shortly.

Not long after, the bank called with a surprising piece of information. Unknown to the couple, the bank had sold their mortgage to another organization and the couple would have to contact the new mortgage holder. The couple dutifully made the call. I can't imagine what they felt with their house hanging by a thread. Keep in mind that the couple kept returning to their Movie every day.

They discovered the new owner of their mortgage was no longer in business! Now what? Who were they supposed to talk to? Who were they supposed to make house payments to?

The couple continued their Movie newly inspired. Within a couple of weeks, they coincidentally met an investigator for a group of lawyers. These lawyers specialized in the problems house owners were having with their mortgage holders. The investigator heard their story, made inquiries and came back with the most amazing news. The couple's mortgage had been sold five more times and was being held by a company in Europe. Here's the best part: The European company didn't have paperwork solidly connecting the company to the mortgage!

A lot of back-and-forth ensued and finally, a court hearing was held in the couple's county. At the hearing, a lawyer representing the European company was called upon to show evidence that the company owned this mortgage. The lawyer presented a computer spreadsheet listing the couple's name along with a number of others as a list. "What is this?" the judge asked. The lawyer replied that the spreadsheet was proof that the company held the mortgage. "My 4-year-old could do this," the judge responded. "You have no standing in my court. Don't come back until you have proper documentation linking you to this mortgage."

At the time of this writing, the couple has been in their house for 2 ½ years without making a mortgage payment. Their case is now part of a larger class-action suit. It's highly likely their case will take some time to resolve, but in the meantime, their businesses are rebounding. Since there is no institution to pay, the couple is still living in their wonderful home and putting what would be the mortgage payment away into their personal savings account.

I asked them how they felt about the turn of events. They replied that what they were experiencing was virtually impossible. They both felt their Movie may have had a lot to do with their situation, since every day they are in their perfect home without a financial hardship. If for whatever reason they lose this home, they feel sure their next home will be equal to or even better than their present house.

As I like to say, they are on the right bus. They have created a specific housing future that is taking them to their perfect conclusion. If it's not this house, it will be another and another until the perfect home presents itself. This optimal house will be ideal physically with the right location and financially comfortable as well.

Here's that phrase again, "Be careful what you ask for." When I feel anxious about a request, I ask anyway but add this comforting phrase,

**"I ask for these things to come with an ease and a grace."**

This book is not about money or possessions; they don't guarantee fulfillment and joy. We live in a physical world bound by an economic system, at least that's the perception. Don't limit yourself by conforming to the common view. Health, happiness and comfort come in a variety of forms.

Don't discount the "equivalent" of money coming your way. You could find that you have to pay less to live or you may come into some unexpected income. There are thousands of money equivalents that can present themselves. The equivalent of money spends just like money.

As you think about what you require, remember that we all know of fabulously wealthy people who are impoverished and unhappy in their hearts. Possessions can bring joy or slavery. Why settle for anything less than your ideal in whatever form it might take? You're looking for your perfect partner? The equivalent of your perfect partner may be you. You may find that perfect companion or you may become perfectly content on your own with a wonderful variety of supporting and entertaining friends.

## More of Your Stories

This is a results-driven book, not speculation, so your success stories are important. A new story from a reader is offered each week in the *Manifesting 1, 2, 3* newsletter and they are also archived at www.manifesting123.com. When you visit the site, sign up for the weekly newsletter, then go to the Story page and see how you can make your dreams come true.

Here are a few stories and my follow-up comments from previous newsletters, all archived on the website.

### $10,000 Redux, Spooky!

*Cindy was reading the Manifesting 1, 2, 3 newsletter from the week before. In the newsletter another reader, Melanie, described how she got her big job offer only hours after making her intention for $10,000. Cindy was moved to take action and she writes:*

It happened all in the same day. In your previous newsletter, I saw the photo of $10,000, and visualized it floating down to me. I thought about how wonderful it would be to ensure that I can cover my house refinance this week. I thought about the stories I've read on your website about manifesting perfect homes, so imagined holding the $10,000 in my hand.

Later the same day, my daughter came to the house, having come straight from her bank with $10,000 cash to give to me! I had sold some jewelry long ago to help pay for her college education. She found out recently that some of her student loans will be forgiven due to unforeseen circumstances, so she wanted to give me $10,000 back.

Such a miracle! And so fast!

—*Cindy*

### Don't Just Wish, CREATE Your Dreams!

In March 2013, I found out I had cancer and went to the Mayo Clinic in Phoenix for treatment. It was a major surgery, but thankfully, they got the cancer in time and I did not need chemo or radiation. The entire ordeal was very serious mentally and physically and I was wiped out.

After the surgery, I arrived home to bad news. The guest cottage I'd rented for 13 years in St. Helena was no longer available. I was told that I had 60 days to move. The cottage is in the Napa Valley and affordable rentals there are incredibly hard to find.

I spoke with Ken and he shared with me his recommendations using *Manifesting 1, 2, 3*. I put it right to work, visualizing the solution in my future.

Luckily I had a friend who let me rent her late mother's furnished house in Napa while I continued to search, literally eight hours a day. During the time I was technically homeless, a big motivator! I had limited time at this temporary rental so I had to really focus. I was taking care of myself and as the book says, I was taking action on my fears, by looking for rentals and doing the manifesting techniques every day. I also have a meditation routine that I kept to. It kept my mind in check and gave me a sense of control and peace.

After two months of looking, I put a deposit on an apartment in a large Napa complex that was dark, old and expensive. It was not what I was looking for but it was all that was available in the area. At least I had secured a place to live.

I continued to use what I had learned about manifesting, visualizing a number of things I desired, including my perfect home. I was not giving up on that!

Soon after, I was driving around the neighborhood and came upon a new complex in St. Helena that had not yet opened. Their certificate of occupancy was stuck in the local bureaucracy and they couldn't give me any hope of when they would open for rentals. Durn!

Then the big break came. Days later I drove by that new complex and to my surprise, the manager was on site with good news. They had just been given the green light to rent the apartments. I was the first one in! Can you believe that? What are the odds of getting the apartment and being first?

It has turned out to be a dream come true. Finally, I have a home with lots of light, a separate office/studio, kitchen, garage, all appliances and everything is brand new. New is PERFECT!

This is so much better than the guest house that I had been in for all of those years. I have created better things than I previously settled for and there is no stopping now. What's the next big thing? I like the idea of my perfect career.

Dreams can come true! Oh yes, and I am soooo very grateful!

—*Sharon*

**Your Checks are in the Mail!**

I lost my corporate job in a layoff over a year ago and I had received the last severance check this past May. I was searching for employment and also researching a business that would be about helping others. I had read *Manifesting 1, 2, 3* and I was using the Movie to create a future where all my expenses and needs are taken care of.

I was at the point where I was going to need more income pretty quick.

Around that time, I was talking to a friend. I was explaining the *Manifesting 1, 2, 3* book to her and talking about how to project your intentions into the future to manifest things. Then it hit me. I remembered something from a film or book where a man went to a mailbox and retrieved envelopes with checks in them. Up to this point, my manifesting scenarios were very general and without visuals.

My friend and I immediately did our Movies together and we felt profound love and gratitude for what we created in our futures. It was the first time I used a visual in my Movie: seeing myself actually getting checks in the mail.

I forgot about it until the next day. I went to my front door just as the mailman was coming up the walk. He handed me a stack of letter-sized envelopes. I knew what they were before I opened them. Unexpected checks! I got goose bumps all over.

The envelopes contained 12 checks! The strange thing was that all 12 checks were from the hospital where I had therapy treatments almost two years before. Those were very expensive treatments mostly covered by insurance, and my co-payment portion was between $150-$200 each session.

This group of checks totaled almost $2,200 and there was no explanation for the refund. It was just a stack of checks without supporting paperwork! It was also odd that I had not received just one check, but multiple checks in separate envelopes. I called the hospital and was transferred around. When I finally got to the right department, the person on the phone couldn't find a record of the checks or the reason I should have them. Finally, a supervisor said that I should just cash them.

This unexpected blessing turned out to be just the right amount for me. I was able to meet my expenses comfortably and I continue to do so now. After that experience, I've been very encouraged to use *Manifesting 1, 2, 3* daily and I have manifested many more things including my perfect career.

My daughter was skeptical of my story, saying that the hospital refund was in progress long before I did the Movie. I personally have had convincing experiences showing me that physical time is not the same as the realm beyond our normal senses. In this other realm, there is no space/time. Regardless of what I think, it doesn't have to make sense. I have clearly seen how thoughts create. It is for me to know and use.

I have had others stories after taking the Manifesting 1, 2, 3 Workshop, but this one with the checks is the most dramatic so far.

This book is brilliant in its simplicity and goes beyond any other manifesting books or techniques I have come across. I have never heard anyone else explain the process of how we manifest before so clearly and simply. It makes perfect sense, and understanding how thought really works makes all the difference. I love the part about addressing concerns or fears by scheduling actions, too. As Ken says, we are already expert at manifesting. So decide on where you want to go and what you desire to do. Be aligned with your true purpose and dreams. Manifesting is incredibly useful and fun!

—*Denae*

*Denae was already using the* Manifesting 1, 2, 3 *techniques but she made two important changes: The first was to create a Movie in which she actually saw the checks she received. Then she infused her scene with emotion and gratitude. I should point out that the solution didn't have to be a check. Financial solutions come in a variety of ways: a reduction in rent, refunds, bonuses and gifts. These are the equivalents of money and they solve financial problems in the same way.*

*When we have a problem fast approaching or surrounding us, it's normal to slide into worry and fear. Denae made the smart move. She envisioned a future where she saw the solution handed to her and she felt a grateful in return.*

## I Hit the Bottom, Then I Made My Plan

I'm a single mom with two kids. I had a beautiful three-bedroom home in a nice part of town. I didn't like my job that much but it paid okay. Then business slumped everywhere and without any fault of mine, I was laid off.

It was an awful time. I had to sell my wonderful house of nine years. That was a blow. The kids and I moved into another place less than one-half the size and they had to share a room.

I was depressed and wasn't sleeping well at all. I did get a job, but in a short time my boss came to me and said I should start looking for another.

I was really up against the wall. I've got a masters degree and I'm just struggling so very hard. I just couldn't get a break. It was bad. I had hit bottom.

I began to think about why I am here. What is it that I want? I'm so ready to get out of this awful position. I decided if I'm going to fall, at least I'm going to fall in the direction of my choosing. If I'm going to fail, then I will fail at something I want to do.

This idea gave me some clarity, so I listed what I wanted to do. It came down to caring for my children, having a fulfilling career and living comfortably.

Then I began a process of slowly letting go of things. I accepted that there might be change and loss. I had some negative distractions in my life, people and things, so I let them go or made healthy adjustments.

Then I began to ask. I decided I would have a career where I would heal people in some way and have a creative life. Health and wellness are important to me and that would be a part of my life as well. I asked to be sustained while I transitioned to my new career.

This was my plan and I went over it every morning and evening.

In the past I had asked for some of these things but my heart was really in it this time. I knew I was worthy to make these requests. My self-worth had been a problem before.

I didn't know if this would work or not, but I couldn't afford lesser options.

I had been told my job was going to end in June. Then my boss left and I was feeling adrift.

Shortly after, the company CEO came to town and asked to have a meeting with me. He said he heard good things about me and asked me to stay. He offered me a promotion and more pay.

It was a stunning turnaround. The promotion required additional responsibilities, so I asked for even more money in line with the new responsibilities. The answer was yes. It was exactly what I needed to stabilize my finances.

I had recently begun a side business out of my home where I'm using my hands and my heart to truly help people. This is the perfect career I was planning for. This business is steadily growing with referrals and new clients. Yes, it takes more of my time, but it doesn't feel like a second job at all. I'm very energized and happy when I'm with my clients, so I'm not fatigued afterwards. It's not a burden at all and I'm building the career of my dreams.

Every day special things happen. I'm meeting wonderful people. Some are teachers for me and in turn, I find myself teaching others more often. There is a lot more synchronicity in my life and all these things confirm that my asking has made a difference.

Looking back, I can see that it all came about because I hit bottom, then asked for a change. I learned to adjust, to be open and ready for whatever happened. It was OK to ask and to dream. I was worthy of happiness.

I learned that we have the power to create and I continue to create my heart's desire. There are many things that I can't control but I navigate onward to my goal.

I consciously let things go, a slow and painful process at times. I gracefully accepted the difficulties that came to my door and stayed with my thoughts and visions for the life I desired. I was visualizing and asking every day with a new heart and a gratefulness that I hadn't felt in a long time.

This has all developed so much better than I had thought and I know it's just the beginning.

At times I'm shocked to see the change. I'm so happy when I sit in my office safe and secure. I have a new optimism. I feel less stress and recently I have even slept in a bit on weekends because my mind is at ease. I find myself saying thank you, thank you, thank you throughout the day.

—*Hannah*

### Dad and Daughter Manifesting Happiness and Breaking Records!

I'm Jessica's dad. My daughter began manifesting after I read Ken's book and gave it to her. We subsequently came to visit Ken because she had some concerns about her competitive swimming.

She had a state swim meet coming up and was really searching for help. She is a young teenager, in middle of a growth spurt that tends to mess with her swimming strokes. She had been mentally down for some time and needed to break the slump.

More than anything, she wanted to smile and have fun. So she envisioned a Movie of herself in the future where she was swimming the best on the biggest stage. She saw herself in the warm-down lanes after her races beaming ear to ear. In her Movie, she did her best and she was very happy.

Well, she stuck to it and visualized this every day. At the state meet she swam her fastest ever, recorded two state times and hit the warm-down pool...for an hour! She was all smiles, ear to ear. She texted me from the pool and it simply said, "He did it," a clear reference to Ken and *Manifesting 1, 2, 3*. I said to her, "No, YOU did it, Mr. Ken just gave you the tools."

As her dad, I was also using those tools to manifest before the meet as well. I was seeing my own Movie in the future where Jessica did her best. I was hugging her after her races and then driving home with her next to me on the front seat. Each day I was manifesting this future where we had our special time in the car after the swimming meet.

Well, it worked! In the car on way home, she leaned over totally exhausted, yet happy as could be. She had her sweatshirt on and pulled up the hood as she lay down next to me. I put my arm around her, just like it was in my Movie. I thought she was sleeping, but then she said out of the blue, "That was so awesome, I want more." Then she zonked out.

It hit me in the heart with a giant thud: I was in tears of joy.

Manifesting works, the Movie is easy for anyone and the rewards are some of the best you will ever experience, materialistic or not.

Go forth and conquer.

—*Dad and Jessica*

*In this story, Jessica did something very wise. She didn't try to manifest a win or set records. Jessica's priority was to smile and have fun. She was open to a larger number of possible outcomes, but they were all happy ones. What wisdom.*

*Jessica is 13 years old. If she can do it and set records in the process, I wonder what you can do?*

### Prayer and Manifesting Prevailed, Not Blindness

I have actually been waiting for about six months to share this information with you. Do you remember when I attended the *Manifesting 1, 2, 3* class in your home last summer? You asked, "What do you want?" and all I could think of was my eyesight. I had glaucoma for about three years at that time.

You told me exactly what to say. You recommended, "I am in my future and my glaucoma does not exist. I am so grateful." Every morning when I woke up I would repeat these exact words. Because I am a Christian, I would also pray for this to happen.

About two to three months later, I went for my annual glaucoma tests. You can imagine my surprise as the doctor was reading my test results and said, "I don't think you have glaucoma."

Frankly, I almost fell out of the chair. I did not want to immediately accept the information. Funny how that works. We ask for a miracle and when it happens we find it difficult to accept.

Anyway, the doctor asked me if I would trust him because for the next six months he wanted me to go off all the medications and then repeat all the tests. Glaucoma develops slowly, so I would be in little danger during this test time.

It has now been six months and I took all of the tests again. I held my breath as he reviewed the test results. He then announced that he was correct and THERE WAS NO EVIDENCE OF GLAUCOMA!!!!

Thank you, Ken. Your book, the exact words you gave me, and the blessings from the Father have changed my life.

—*Your friend, T.*

*The doctor said it was a miracle.*

*T. is an artist and she had been suffering from blind spots for some time. Once she was diagnosed, she began taking medications that required her to sit upright in bed. Her eyesight was deteriorating. She was working with three doctors and T. was told that this particular type of glaucoma usually resulted in blindness.*

*That is a big burden and it would be a lot of worry for most of us. T. moved forward and used all that was at her disposal: her doctors, prayers and manifesting. She was allowing and asking.*

*What amazing news! Her doctor told her that this particular form of glaucoma is rarely cured. When she told her doctor about the book, he advised her to let me know about her good results.*

*I am privileged to hear amazing stories from you all, but this one compelled me to just sit down in quiet gratefulness.*

*There is another hero in this story: her husband. I have in my notes from last year this email snippet from T. regarding last year's* Manifesting 1, 2, 3 *workshop. "My dear husband knows how much I enjoy your company and this topic. He said we will manage the* Manifesting 1, 2, 3 *class fee." We are all so happy she attended!*

*Ask. Show up. Point yourself to happiness. Be grateful to the God of your understanding.*

### Amazingly, I Got the Dream Job!

I have a young, adult son. He's 22. By nature, he's one of the most pessimistic people I know. But hey, it takes all kinds, right? The optimist builds the airplane and the pessimist builds the parachute.

He has been out of college since May and looking for a specific kind of computer programming job. I have heard him rant many times that no one will hire him because he had no experience, and how is he supposed to get experience if no one will hire him? It was a vicious circle of negativity every time I tried to get him to look for a job. He never once finished an application for any job at all.

Finally, after months of frustration, I asked him to sit down with me and do a manifesting Movie. He rolled his eyes, but did it because he loves me. I made him repeat after me, "I am in my future and I'm in my dream job and it looks like this..."

With some prompting, he imagined that he was working with colleagues who treated him with courtesy, humor and respect. Together, he imagined they were creating meaningful work and having a positive impact on his industry and the world at large, and that felt really good.

We talked about how exciting it was to work with like-minded people, and how rewarding it was to produce award-winning work that one could be proud of. We explored that perfect job from every angle. Then we said a great big THANK YOU to everyone, known and unknown, who helped make that future happen.

So two weeks ago he smirked and said, "And this is supposed to help me how?" I explained his manifesting Movie specified the point for his future, and now energy could begin to move. He was skeptical. Very skeptical.

After a week of doing the Movie together, I finally understood what kind of "computer job" he was looking for. I stumbled on an entry-level job online that was perfect and shared it with him.

I have never seen a kid move so fast to get his resume together, get up, dressed, cleaned, shaved, ready for the workplace. He had his very first job interview and he did really well. He was optimistic and upbeat, and sure that this was work worth doing.

Alas, he didn't get that job. That was a bit of a bummer but he did get beneficial experience! He got his cover letter done, his resume compiled, he navigated the interview process successfully and his mental state was ready for work.

Yesterday, he got a call from a former teacher who overheard a colleague talking about someone hiring in my son's very specialized field. She passed along my son's name, and within hours, he had a phone interview with two brothers who are creating a sequel to a very popular mobile app game. He really bonded with the guys and starts work next week making over $50,000 a year! Amazingly, it is an entry-level position in a small company that matches the characteristics specified in his manifesting Movie! Incredible!

I know that this NEVER would have happened if we hadn't done his manifesting Movie In fact, I believe that neither of us could even IMAGINE this job before. Just by using the *Manifesting 1, 2, 3* Movie process ONE TIME ONLY, his pessimistic points of view were replaced with positive, peaceful possibilities. And voila, his Movie manifested! A perfect job came along, AND he was looking for it, AND he could recognize it AND he believes that he can do great work!

Creating his manifesting Movie allowed my son to open up and let something really great slip in. No longer does he believe that "No one will hire me. I don't have experience. I'll hate working with other people." He's on his way to a successful, meaningful adulthood.

Ken, I cannot thank you enough for writing your book, and sharing it with the world. You are making a big difference for so many people. My son and I will be forever grateful.

—*Jane*


*No experience was necessary! Jane and her son get all the credit. What a wonderful outcome. It is difficult to explain that with a little* effort on your part, wonderful things can be brought to you.

Jane's son was a skeptic and not the Pollyanna type, but he used his thoughts to create a future of his making anyway.

This story is a great example, showing that anyone can point themselves to what makes them happy. Belief, faith and special skills are not required. Congratulations on the great new job and way to go, Mom. Don't stop now!

## Manifesting Colorado via Las Vegas!

I visited Colorado for business and instantly fell in love with the beauty that the state had to offer and all the wonderful people there. While I was in Colorado, I kept thinking to myself, how nice it would be to live here. Logically, this would be very difficult to say or certainly do.

I was in the middle of a major career transition and money was an issue, not to mention finding a place to live when I currently resided several states away. When I returned to my home state, I prepared the way and put into practice what I had learned from Ken Elliott for manifesting a move to Colorado. I had no idea how I was going to come up with the money, how to do it, or how it was going to happen. I knew in my heart that it was going to happen.

It wasn't long after that I had an opportunity to travel back to Colorado for business. This time I decided to drive and spend the night in Las Vegas, making the two-day trip more manageable. All the way, I was playing my Movie and I could see my life in Colorado as if it was already happening.

I arrived in Vegas after 5 p.m., checked in to my hotel room and after dinner decided to play a little on the slot machines. I'm not a big gambler, so this was just for fun and something to pass the time. It wasn't long however, (a whopping 10 minutes max!) that all of the lights on my slot machine lit up. I had just won $5,000! After collecting my winnings, I went back to my hotel room.

I was overcome with gratitude. I knew that all of that talk about "running your Movie" that I had learned in *Manifesting 1, 2, 3* had now manifested the money that I needed to make my move and then some! I now live blissfully in the state that I love, surrounded by people who add so much joy and fulfillment to my life!

I feel so blessed!

Thank you, Universe!

—*Joyce*

*Not the plan: Well, kinda...*

*Joyce had a plan. Well, not really, but she was pointing herself to Colorado using the manifesting technique of her Movie and imagining she was already there. Moving to Colorado was going to be complicated. She would need a new job, a place to live and somehow pay for the change.*

*She stayed with the idea and continued the manifesting techniques until the solution arrived. She didn't plan on gambling her way to a solution, it just fell into her lap one day - in 10 minutes!*

*Just to be clear, let's not all run off to Vegas and gamble as a business plan. On the other hand, if a large amount of money or the equivalent of money suddenly falls into your lap and it solves a current problem, then it's a great day!*

## Can Anyone Manifest a Big List? Read On

Recently I wanted to go to a conference in Utah but getting the money and time off from my husband's job was a big problem.

To make things worse, my car was no longer drivable. It was the engine and it was looking like a full replacement. My husband's car needed repairs as well, but at least they were less expensive. He was just being practical when he said we can go on the trip or fix the car, but not both.

I have a couple of good friends, Dave and Carol. They told me if you want something, ask for it.

Then I thought back to a conference I attended in Kansas City. Ken Elliott was introducing his new book, *Manifesting 1, 2, 3* to the large audience there. It certainly made an impact on the audience and me - he got a standing ovation. It all made perfect sense and I went with it for a time before I stopped using *Manifesting 1, 2, 3* as a daily practice.

After talking with Dave and Carol, I went to the *Manifesting 1, 2, 3* website to review Ken's radio interviews. I like his philosophy: everything you need is there in the interviews for free. No teasers or gimmicks. I had a lot that I wanted solved in a very short time. "How is this possibly going to work?" I thought, but I went for it.

*Manifesting 1, 2, 3* changed my life.

I wanted to go to the Utah conference and my husband added if we were going to drive that kind of distance, then we should be doing a real vacation. Okay, as long as I'm manifesting this, let's have the money for the conference and the long trip as a package. Why not?

Right away, things started falling into place.

The closer the conference date came, the more I felt things change. Surprisingly, my husband got two weeks off. Then we were able to get his jeep repaired. We could repair only one of our two vehicles, but now we had a dependable car for our road trip.

Soon after, I had a friend that passed, but quite unexpectedly, a small amount of money was willed to me. It was enough to pay for our real vacation and the conference.

Off we went! Starting at our home in Wisconsin, we first visited Mount Rushmore and went on to the conference in Utah. At the conference there were people that knew of my work as a spiritual practitioner. I did a number of personal sessions there and received more funds for our vacation.

We had a National Parks pass, so we left Utah and went to the Grand Canyon. Our last scheduled destination was Tombstone Arizona where my husband visited his father's burial site. Amazingly, I made some new friends in Tombstone and I'm getting new business from that pleasant encounter.

It was quite a trip and we went through the Big Corn Patch attraction on our trip as well. Time and money was not a concern. What a relief.

After returning from our trip I continued to stay with my *Manifesting 1, 2, 3* routine. On my manifesting list was to somehow get some dental work done. I have some teeth missing so this is a real priority. A solution arrived in the form of free dental care! It seems miraculous.

Things are just getting better. I'm not the same person anymore. I am happier and even ecstatic at times. Every morning I wake up with a smile on my face.

I've talked to my husband about manifesting. We are both changing. We have more mutual goals than ever before. My husband notices these things. All of a sudden our lives are moving forward so smoothly.

It just keeps coming.

Somehow I got a new motor for my pickup, cheap! It now runs like brand new. In my Movie I am manifesting checks and they show up - much more than before.

I am sharing all I know to my clients and friends.

I'm tickled and so thankful!

Oh yes, I'm doing my Movie every day.

     Bless your heart,

     —*Cindy*


These letters are wonderful, and here is a something unexpected, a delightful side-effect that many have reported.

There is a common theme coming in from readers of *Manifesting*

*1, 2, 3.* It goes something like this: They typically close their eyes and visualize their future each day as a Movie and in their future, life is good! Their current problems don't exist in this future. In their future vision they observe how everything worked out and their dreams and aspirations have already happened.

In their future, they experience a lot of gratefulness and worry or fear is not to be found. In these Movies, comfort, happiness and peace are the norm.

Now their Movie is done and they open their eyes to the real world with the ups and downs typical to everyone. No fantasy here. The schedule awaits and the everyday pressures and demands start to sink in. Or do they?

People are reporting that after they have done the *Manifesting 1, 2, 3* for a time, something unusual happens: Out of the blue, they just wake up happier. It just happens. After days and weeks of spending time in their happy Movie future, happiness finds them. How?

It could be any number of things; all good. After spending hours in that lovely future, they experience a pleasant respite from the everyday world, much like the after-effect of watching a happy film at the local cinema.

It could also be that they have the equivalent of one foot in the future at all times and a pleasant connection is made to the Now. Others observe that so many of their future scenes have come to pass that they often experience their future now.

Whatever the cause may be, this happiness effect is very common and a sweet surprise. Here's another after-effect: A number of other people, some very successful businesspeople, talk about something more. They notice that the problems common to their jobs are somehow diminished. The problems are still there—work is like that—but for whatever reason, these troubles don't get under their skin and aggravate them as much.

Readers commonly mention that it is as if they are operating on some higher level. Somehow these common problems seem less compelling because they have a higher or wiser point of view. They love it. The tasks flow easier, there is less stress and their jobs become more pleasurable.

### Why would we be surprised to wake up happy?

Perhaps it is because we have been trained to think that it can't be that easy. We are not deserving. It is not our turn or fate to be happy and comfortable. Or some say they have never really been happy, so this is not going to be possible.

### Well, it happens anyway.

They didn't sign up for the Happiness Seminar or take the happy pill. Each person simply used the techniques in the book. They went to the future, expressed gratefulness and off-loaded the fears that would block their progress. It was so very easy and pleasurable to do.

## Last Thoughts

Is life not going your way?

Are you overburdened with problems and personal issues?

Is your relationship a mess?

**I will gently offer that most of the responsibility falls on you.**

For the most part, you have decided to be right where you are. You have brought yourself to this point of being happy or miserable. Some of life is inescapable but everything else is a response to the choices you make. You have been empowered since birth to create. You have been creating all your life.

Whatever position you are in today, it's alright. It's alright. Perhaps nobody told you what you can do. Maybe you never heard it enough or in just the right way about the great gift you have to create anything.

You have a new future beginning in one minute. You now have a way out, a method to change the arc of your life. Fifty seconds now. Every minute is an opportunity to make a new future. Forty seconds now.

I hope that you'll be inclined to use the information in this book to better your life and go where you want to go.

Be wise, you now have one of the keys to the kingdom.

Point yourself to happiness.

Be good to yourself.

# My Notes

Grab a pen or pencil and start now. Add your thoughts to the pages here or write your thoughts in a private journal.

I am in my future and I am:
(Avoid words like need or want. Describe the things in your future that have already happened.)

What is currently in my present that will NOT be in my future:
(My present attitude, unhappiness, negative environment, lack, etc)

In my future I'm happy because:
(What is in the way of your happiness now? What are the situations, present beliefs and blocks?)

In my future I am feeling:
(Make it good!)

How can I most efficiently describe the items in my future Movie? (Some scenes in your Movie will have detail and you will use many of your senses. For concepts like health, you may observe you are healthy from the couch in your perfect home or during a wonderful vacation. You may envision a perfect career without being in an office or at a desk working.)

What can I do now to be more joyful?
(Are you presently happy at your core? If not, do the seven Grateful
Things every day. Also, write down what would make you happier now
and don't worry about how it could possibly occur. What can you presently do to reduce your stress and worry?)

What should I place on my Wish List?
(The sky is the limit! You are creating as you write this.)

What should I put on my Vision Board?
(These are the pictures that represent what you want to see in your future every day.)

My seven Grateful Things:
(What are the good things in your life? List more than seven if you like.
Include joyful events from your past to make way for more to come.)

## Resources

William Buhlman is the foremost writer on the subject of out-of-body or astral travel and his books have been translated into eight languages. William is the author of *Adventures Beyond the Body* and *Secrets of the Soul*. His web site is www.astralinfo.org.

Judy Goodman, CPC, CSRC, CRC, is a professional coach, counselor, hypnotherapist and a highly recognized intuitive. Her web site is www.judygoodman.com. Her email is JudyKGoodman@aol.com.

# Acknowledgements

I want to thank my editor, Janice Brewster, for her diligence and professionalism. Her guidance, clarity and light touch kept this book in my own voice and made it far better than I could have written on my own. To Karen Sulmonetti, I offer my sincere appreciation for taking my manuscript and fashioning an artful interior for all who read it. Her cover designs brought it all together and made my wishes come true.

Then there is Mike Daniels, The Publisher's Coach, who guided me to the all-pro team at Frederic Printing that helped bring this book to life, thank you!
My gratitude to the great fiber artist Carol Ann Waugh for her wisdom.
www.carolannwaugh.com

Additionally, Melissa Glueck and Susan Buhlman read through the manuscript versions and offered helpful advice that was used here. Thank you both so very much. Together, everyone urged me to more fully describe some of the concepts mentioned here and aided the order and easy flow of the book. I am so very grateful. Once the book is done another phase begins. I want to happily acknowledge Marianne Pestana for her social media expertise and unwavering support. www.mariannepestana.com.

I want to thank you, the reader as well. It is my honor to share this time with you. All that is contained here was gifted to me and I'm passing it on to you. Should this book give you comfort then I hope you will offer it forward as well.

Photography: Marianne Pestana

# ABOUT THE AUTHOR

Ken Elliott is an author and artist living in Castle Rock, Colorado. He has experienced and collected astonishing stories for more than 25 years. In a unique and convincing way, Ken learned how thought works, continually building objects and concepts in the unseen field around each of us. Ken is an accomplished speaker, passing this empowering information on to individuals and groups. For more information on Ken's lectures and workshops, email ken@manifesting123.com or visit www.manifesting123.com. To see Ken's artworks, visit www.kenelliott.com.

# Manifesting Made Simple

Your thoughts begin to take form immediately in the unseen field around you.
Make time every day to use your thoughts in this powerful and efficient way.

### 1 Go into your Movie and imagine you are in your future.

Go for perfect with little detail or use a lot. Be in your Movie, explore your senses
and be grateful in every scene. Don't consider how the scenes in your Movie came
about. Leave out what you don't want.

### 2 Worries are thoughts, too.

Worries are powered by fear and create negative outcomes. Convert your worries
to calendar or action items that are not emotionally loaded. Replace words like
"going to" with "doing" or "I am moving toward..."

### 3 You have never been more powerful.

Don't try to be powerful in your Movie, it will just get in your way.
Just be as a child and be in your Movie without judgement.

## Bonus!

Think of 7 Grateful Things every day.
Make the way clear for your happiness.
Thank God or the God of your understanding for all you are grateful for.

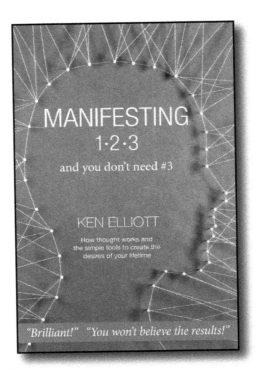

Available in paperback or ebook at Amazon.com, and other outlets. For a copy signed by the author ($14.95 plus shipping), visit www.manifesting123.com.

Ken Elliott is an author and artist living in Castle Rock, Colorado. He has experienced and collected astonishing stories for more than 25 years. In a unique and convincing way, Ken learned how thought works, continually building objects and concepts in the unseen field around each of us. Ken is an accomplished speaker, passing this empowering information on to individuals and groups. For more information on Ken's lectures and workshops, email ken@manifesting123.com or visit www.manifesting123.com.

